YORK NOTES

Wuthering Heights

Emily Brontë

Notes by Andrew Pierce

Longman   York Press

YORK PRESS
322 Old Brompton Road, London SW5 9JH

ADDISON WESLEY LONGMAN LIMITED
Edinburgh Gate, Harlow,
Essex CM20 2JE, United Kingdom
Associated companies, branches and representatives throughout the world

First published 1998

ISBN 0–582–36845–6

Designed by Vicki Pacey, Trojan Horse, London
Illustrated by Gerry Grace
Phototypeset by Gem Graphics, Trenance, Mawgan Porth, Cornwall
Colour reproduction and film output by Spectrum Colour
Produced by Addison Wesley Longman China Limited, Hong Kong

CONTENTS

PREFACE

York Notes are designed to give you a broader perspective on works of literature studied at GCSE and equivalent levels. We have carried out extensive research into the needs of the modern literature student prior to publishing this new edition. Our research showed that no existing series fully met students' requirements. Rather than present a single authoritative approach, we have provided alternative viewpoints, empowering students to reach their own interpretations of the text. York Notes provide a close examination of the work and include biographical and historical background, summaries, glossaries, analyses of characters, themes, structure and language, cultural connections and literary terms.

If you look at the Contents page you will see the structure for the series. However, there's no need to read from the beginning to the end as you would with a novel, play, poem or short story. Use the Notes in the way that suits you. Our aim is to help you with your understanding of the work, not to dictate how you should learn.

York Notes are written by English teachers and examiners, with an expert knowledge of the subject. They show you how to succeed in coursework and examination assignments, guiding you through the text and offering practical advice. Questions and comments will extend, test and reinforce your knowledge. Attractive colour design and illustrations improve clarity and understanding, making these Notes easy to use and handy for quick reference.

York Notes are ideal for:
- Essay writing
- Exam preparation
- Class discussion

The author of these Notes is Andrew Pierce MA, B Phil, MA (Educ), who is an Examiner for A level English for a major examination board. Born in Keighley, and educated at the Universities of Cambridge, York and London, he has taught in a range of grammar and comprehensive schools, and Tertiary Colleges.

The edition used in these Notes is the Longman Literature Edition, edited by Celeste Flower, 1991.

Health Warning: **This study guide will enhance your understanding, but should not replace the reading of the original text and/or study in class.**

PART ONE

INTRODUCTION

HOW TO STUDY A NOVEL

You have bought this book because you wanted to study
a novel on your own. This may supplement classwork.

- You will need to read the novel several times. Start by
  reading it quickly for pleasure, then read it slowly and
  carefully. Further readings will generate new ideas
  and help you to memorise the details of the story.
- Make careful notes on themes, plot and characters of
  the novel. The plot will change some of the
  characters. Who changes?
- The novel may not present events chronologically.
  Does the novel you are reading begin at the
  beginning of the story or does it contain flashbacks
  and a muddled time sequence? Can you think why?
- How is the story told? Is it narrated by one of the
  characters or by an all-seeing ('omniscient') narrator?
- Does the same person tell the story all the way
  through? Or do we see the events through the minds
  and feelings of a number of different people.
- Which characters does the narrator like? Which
  characters do you like or dislike? Do your sympathies
  change during the course of the book? Why? When?
- Any piece of writing (including your notes and
  essays) is the result of thousands of choices. No book
  had to be written in just one way: the author could
  have chosen other words, other phrases, other
  characters, other events. How could the author of
  your novel have written the story differently? If events
  were recounted by a minor character how would this
  change the novel?

Studying on your own requires self-discipline and a
carefully thought-out work plan in order to be effective.
Good luck.

Less is known about Emily Brontë than her brother and sisters. The glimpses we have of her (based partly on rumour and her sister Charlotte's writings) make a fascinating picture. You might not be surprised at her habit of lying on the floor in front of the fire reading, nor at her love of animals, but there are also reports of her cauterising herself with a red-hot iron after being bitten by a dog, and learning to shoot her father's pistol.

Childhood

Born in 1818 at Thornton in Yorkshire, Emily Brontë lived for most of her life at Haworth, near Keighley. The fifth of the six children of Reverend Patrick Brontë, she became familiar with death early. When she was three years old in 1821, her mother died of cancer, and when she was seven her two elder sisters, boarding at Cowan Bridge School, died of consumption. Emily and her sister Charlotte, who also attended this school, returned to Haworth where, with their sister Anne and brother Branwell, they were brought up by their aunt. Emily was apparently an intelligent, lively child, becoming more reserved as she grew older.

Being separated from someone you love is a central theme in Wuthering Heights.

Childhood writings

In their close-knit family, the Brontë children created a fantasy world. This was partly inspired by a box of toy soldiers Patrick gave Branwell in 1826. The children invented names and countries for them, with Emily and Anne creating the land of Gondal. The characters developed and changed, and the Brontës wrote stories about them. Emily later wrote Gondal poems set in a landscape like Haworth's, with characters and themes which anticipate *Wuthering Heights* (see Broader Perspectives).

The seeds of Wuthering Heights can be found in Emily's early writings.

1835–42 Away from home: studying and teaching

During these years, Emily left home three times to equip herself to make a living as a teacher. Aged 17, she briefly attended Roe Head School but was so homesick that she was physically ill. In 1837, she became a governess in a girls' boarding school at Law Hill near Halifax. She wrote poetry here, but after six months her health broke down and she returned home. Thinking to start their own school, Emily and Charlotte went to study in Brussels in 1842. However, that October, their aunt died, and they returned home. Their school never opened.

1842–8
Haworth:
domestic duties
and writing

After this, Emily remained at Haworth, looking after her father and the household. She continued writing, and in 1846, persuaded by Charlotte, the sisters published a joint collection of poems, under the pen names of Currer, Ellis and Acton Bell. *Wuthering Heights,* probably begun in autumn 1845, was published in December 1847. Reviews were mixed. The novel's power and originality were recognised, but fault was found with its violence, coarse language, and apparent lack of a moral.

In September 1848, Branwell, whose various attempts at making a career ended in addiction to opium and drink, died. After his funeral, Emily became ill but, refusing a doctor, carried on with her household duties. She died on 19 December 1848 of consumption, with characteristic courage and independence of spirit. Charlotte wrote in the 1850 edition of *Wuthering Heights*:

> Day by day, when I saw with what a front she met suffering, I looked on her with anguish of wonder and love. I have seen nothing like it; but, indeed, I have never seen her parallel in anything. Stronger than a man, simpler than a child, her nature stood alone.

GEOGRAPHICAL

The setting of the novel is influenced by the area where Emily Brontë lived.

Haworth parsonage stands above the town, next to the graveyard and on the edge of the moors. The deep love Emily Brontë had for the wildness and freedom of the moors is shown in her vivid descriptions of a landscape that is affected by the seasons and changes in weather.

Her ideas for Wuthering Heights and Thrushcross Grange are probably partly based on buildings near Haworth: High Withins, a farm on the moors, and Ponden Hall lower in the valley. There are two other houses, High Sunderland and Shibden Hall, near where Emily taught at Law Hill, Halifax, which are similarly situated. At Law Hill, Emily also heard the legend of Jack Sharp, an orphan like Heathcliff, who was adopted by a local landowner, and eventually took over his property.

SOCIAL AND POLITICAL

It is a myth that Emily Brontë lived in romantic isolation, cut off from the rest of society.

Emily Brontë lived in a time of social change and unrest, and would have seen evidence of this around her in Haworth. Although close to the moors, Haworth was a large industrial village, near to the centre of the woollen industry. With the coming of machinery, many local people, who had combed wool by hand in their own cottages, had no work. The Poor Law (criticised by Charles Dickens in *Oliver Twist*) meant that to receive assistance people had to live in a workhouse which often involved the break-up of families. Because of poverty, starvation and insanitary conditions, between 1838 and 1849 (when Emily was writing *Wuthering Heights*), over 40% of children in Haworth died before the age of six.

This caused considerable unrest, including riots in nearby towns sometimes leading to the use of troops.

The Chartist movement, campaigning for electoral
reform, held huge meetings on the moors, and Patrick
Brontë himself took part in public meetings in
Haworth supporting reform and attacking the Poor
Law.

Wuthering Heights, set at the end of the eighteenth
century, does not portray the contemporary situation
directly. However, the novel does reflect social tension
and conflict. In 1845, when Emily was writing the
novel, Branwell returned from Liverpool having seen
recently arrived victims of the Irish famine, starving in
the streets. Interestingly, Heathcliff is originally found
starving on the streets of Liverpool, speaking an
unintelligible language. He is then branded, by Hindley
and the Lintons, as a social inferior and a threat to their
property. Separated from his love by those with social
privilege, he avenges himself by making money, and
gaining control of the property of those who have
oppressed him.

RELIGIOUS

*The belief that
sinners deserved
eternal
punishment in
Hell was
widespread.*

Emily Brontë met authoritarian, unforgiving forms of
Christianity both as a pupil at Cowan Bridge School,
where the Reverend Carus Wilson read stories about
children struck down by God for being naughty, and in
the likes of Reverend Jabez Bunting, a local Methodist
who refused funeral rites to those involved in riots. In
her novel, we meet similarly harsh religious views,
based on sin and punishment, in the form of Reverend
Jabez Branderham (in Lockwood's dream) and
Joseph. The rebelliousness shown by Catherine and
Heathcliff surely reflects Emily Brontë's own. The
inadequacy of rigid judgemental attitudes is shown in
her novel.

Literary

In Patrick Brontë's library, Emily came across such
works as Bunyan's *Pilgrim's Progress* (Heathcliff refers to
its Slough of Despond in Chapter 22) and Milton's
Paradise Lost (whose Satan some see as resembling
Heathcliff). As far as contemporary writers go, she was
familiar with the work of Byron (1788–1824), whose
glamorous, criminal heroes have similarities with
Heathcliff. She was also an admirer of Sir Walter Scott
(1771–1832), whose *Rob Roy* (1817) contains characters
which recall hers, and would have come across **Gothic
horror stories** (see Literary Terms) in Blackwood's
Magazine. As important as any literary influence,
however, was the oral tradition of folk tales and ballads,
containing such themes as revenge and family enmity
(Cathy refers to 'Chevy Chase'), or dead lovers coming
at night to their love's window, (as in a ballad like 'The
Grey Cock'). Emily had access to these through the
family servant, Tabby, who is sometimes seen as a
model for Nelly Dean and, indeed, an influence on the
narrative technique of the novel.

PART TWO

SUMMARIES

To avoid confusion between the heroines, the older Catherine is referred to throughout these Notes as Catherine, and her daughter (the younger Catherine) as Cathy.

GENERAL SUMMARY

Chapters 1–3: Wuthering Heights has visitors	In November 1801, a gentleman from the south of England, Mr Lockwood, arrives at Wuthering Heights, a lonely old farmhouse on the Yorkshire moors. He meets the owner, Mr Heathcliff, from whom he is renting Thrushcross Grange. Puzzled by the hostile behaviour of the house's inhabitants, he makes a series of wrong assumptions about them. That night, forced to stay by a snowstorm, he has a terrifying dream involving a ghost.
Chapters 4–9: Childhood and separation	Back at Thrushcross Grange, Lockwood asks his housekeeper, Nelly Dean, about Heathcliff. Nelly explains how, in 1771, Heathcliff, as a child, was rescued from the Liverpool slums by her old master, Mr Earnshaw. Heathcliff became close to Earnshaw's daughter, Catherine, but was hated by his son, Hindley. When Earnshaw died, Hindley treated Heathcliff as a servant, depriving him of education, and instilling in him a desire for revenge.
	When Catherine met Edgar Linton, from Thrushcross Grange, she was attracted by his wealth and social position. Although Heathcliff resented this relationship, Catherine agreed to marry Edgar, assuming it would not affect her relationship with Heathcliff. One night, Heathcliff overheard her say the reason she would not marry him was because it would degrade her. He disappeared into the night.
Chapters 10–17: The return of Heathcliff	Three years later, Heathcliff returned to find Catherine and Edgar married. Heathcliff was transformed into a gentleman with money. Catherine was overjoyed to see him and expected Edgar to accept him. However,

Heathcliff's return created tension between Catherine and Edgar. The situation worsened when Edgar's sister, Isabella, became infatuated with Heathcliff. Heathcliff disliked her, but was interested that she was Edgar's heir. After a violent confrontation, in which Catherine sided with Heathcliff, Edgar issued an ultimatum: she must choose between them. Catherine shut herself in her room, refusing food, and became ill.

Heathcliff then eloped with Isabella. Catherine seemed to recover until, three months later, he returned. After a passionate scene of mutual accusation, she died, having given birth to Cathy. At her death, Heathcliff prayed that she haunt him for the rest of his life. Isabella, now full of hatred for Heathcliff, escaped from the Heights, fleeing South where she had a son, Linton. Meanwhile, Hindley's drinking and gambling had ruined his health. Having mortgaged the Heights, he died in debt. Heathcliff gained control of both the house and Hindley's son, Hareton.

Chapters 18–28: The second generation

Twelve years passed. Nelly describes how young Cathy, aged thirteen, went by herself to the moors. She visited Wuthering Heights, having met Hareton who, because of his degradation by Heathcliff, she mistook for a servant.

Shortly afterwards, Isabella died. Edgar brought Linton to the Grange, but Heathcliff, as his father, claimed him and took him to Wuthering Heights. Heathcliff planned that Linton and Cathy should marry, to strengthen his claim to the Lintons' property on Edgar's death. So he enticed Cathy, now sixteen, to the Heights. She took pity on the sickly, selfish Linton and, thinking she loved him, wrote to him secretly.

Edgar's health declined and death approached. Caught

between loyalty to her father, who had forbidden visits to the Heights, and pity for Linton, Cathy was unable to resist Heathcliff luring her there as part of his plan of revenge. Eventually, just as Edgar was dying, Heathcliff succeeded in trapping Cathy, refusing to release her until she had married Linton. Cathy did marry Linton, and escaped from the Heights just before her father died. However, Heathcliff now controlled not only Wuthering Heights but also all the Lintons' property.

Chapters
29–34:
An end and a
beginning

Heathcliff forced Cathy to return to Wuthering Heights. He told Nelly how, after Edgar's funeral, he broke into Catherine's coffin and saw her corpse. He also revealed that after her funeral, nearly eighteen years before, he uncovered her coffin but was stopped from breaking in by a sense of her presence which led him back to the Heights. To his frustration, she didn't actually appear to him but this sense of her presence had haunted him ever since. Linton then died and Cathy, isolated and numbed by Linton's death, rejected Hareton's friendship.

Lockwood visits the Heights to tell Heathcliff he is leaving the Grange. He sees Hareton and Cathy quarrelling and a change in Heathcliff.

Later in 1802, Lockwood returns. He hears about Heathcliff's death and the events preceding it. He learns how Hareton and Cathy became lovers, and are to be married on New Year's Day, also how Heathcliff's behaviour changed before his death and how he lost his desire for revenge. He was buried, as he wished, next to Catherine, but since his death, local people claim to have seen them together. As Lockwood leaves, he passes their peaceful graves, telling himself they must finally be at rest.

	1757	Hindley Earnshaw born
	1762	Edgar Linton born
	1764	Heathcliff born
	1765	Catherine Earnshaw and Isabella Linton born
Chapter 4	**1771**	*Summer* Heathcliff brought to Wuthering Heights
Chapter 5	**1774**	*Autumn* Hindley sent to College
	1777	Hindley marries Frances
Chapter 5		*October* Mr Earnshaw dies;
Chapter 6		Hindley returns;
Chapter 3		Scene described in Catherine's diary
Chapter 6		*November* Heathcliff and Catherine visit the Grange
Chapter 7		*December 24* Catherine returns
Chapter 7		*December 25* Lintons visit the Heights
Chapter 8	**1778**	*June* Hareton Earnshaw born; Frances dies
Chapter 9	**1780**	*Summer* Heathcliff leaves
		April Catherine and Edgar marry
Chapter 10	**1783**	*September* Heathcliff returns
Chapter 11	**1784**	*January* Edgar and Heathcliff quarrel;
Chapter 11		Catherine refuses food
Chapter 12		Isabella and Heathcliff elope

Chapter **13**		**March** Isabella and Heathcliff return to the Heights
Chapter **15**		**March 19** Passionate scene between Heathcliff and Catherine
Chapter **16**		**March 20** Cathy born; Catherine dies
Chapter **17**		**March 25** Isabella escapes
Chapter **18** Chapter **19** Chapter **20**	1797	**Summer** Cathy visits the Heights, meeting Hareton; Isabella dies; Edgar returns with Linton; Heathcliff takes Linton to the Heights
Chapter **21**	1800	**March 20** Cathy meets Heathcliff and visits the Heights
Chapter **27**	1801	**August** Cathy marries Linton
Chapter **28** Chapter **29**		**September** Edgar dies Cathy taken to the Heights
Chapter **30**		**October** Linton dies
Chapters **1,2,3** Chapter **4**		**November** Lockwood visits the Heights; reads diary; sees ghost Lockwood is ill; Nelly begins Heathcliff's story
Chapter **31**	1802	**January** Lockwood leaves for London
Chapter **32**		**March** Relationship of Cathy and Hareton develops
Chapter **34**		**May** Heathcliff dies
Chapters **32-4**		**September** Lockwood returns and is brought up to date by Nelly
Chapter **34**	1803	**January 1** Cathy and Hareton to marry

Detailed Summaries

CHAPTER 1   Mr Lockwood, having rented Thrushcross Grange in Yorkshire, describes in his diary (dated 1801) a visit to his landlord, Mr Heathcliff, at Wuthering Heights.

Notice how Emily Brontë uses detail to create atmosphere (see Literary Terms), outside and inside the house.

Lockwood finds Heathcliff and his servant, Joseph, unfriendly. The house itself is also unwelcoming; its surroundings have suffered neglect and exposure to the elements. However, Lockwood is intrigued by carvings over the door. He is also curious about Heathcliff and undeterred by his 'reserve'. Lockwood thinks he has found a kindred spirit, revealing that he himself wants to get away from the world to recover from an encounter with a girl he met that summer. He found her 'fascinating' but when she returned his affection, he broke off the relationship.

Left in a room full of dogs, he is attacked. After being rescued, he leaves, intending to return next day.

COMMENT   Lockwood is one of the main **narrators** (see Literary Terms and Structure); he is observant and provides a detailed description. He is also a character (see Characters) whose attitudes and behaviour add to the meaning of the novel. From the start, we question his judgement that he and Heathcliff are similar.

Does his comment on the dialect (see Literary Terms) word 'Wuthering' (p. 2) seem pompous?

Lockwood's language shows he is educated and civilised (see Language and Style). He uses **Latinate** (see Literary Terms) words like 'perseverance' and 'soliciting', and distances himself from his seaside relationship by quoting Shakespeare.

The gate acts as a 'barrier'; corners are 'defended' (p. 2).

The language used to describe Wuthering Heights suggests its hostility. Inside, there are 'hidden dens' haunted by fierce dogs. The description of the 'assault' on Lockwood as a 'tempest' or 'storm' (p. 5), recalls the house's name and the violent natural forces which assail it (e.g. in Chapter 9).

Heathcliff's uncivilised aggressiveness is shown by his behaviour and the language which describes him. Notice, for example, words linking Heathcliff with both house and dogs.

GLOSSARY

Wuthering stormy (Yorkshire dialect – see Literary Terms)

craving alms of the sun the thorn trees are like paupers begging for charity

penetralium the innermost part of the house (Latin)

underdrawn covered with boards and plaster

never told my love hid my feelings (*Twelfth Night* II.4.109)

set my signet on the biter had one of the dogs actually bitten him, his signet ring would have left a mark where he had struck it

CHAPTER 2

Lockwood comically mistakes a heap of dead rabbits for cats.

He noticed this name carved over the entrance to the house in Chapter 1.

Lockwood returns to a bleak, unwelcoming Wuthering Heights and gets everything wrong. He meets a rough-looking young man, then an attractive, unfriendly girl whom he mistakes for Heathcliff's wife. Lockwood then assumes the girl must be married to the young man, whom he finds 'bordering on repulsive' (p. 11). However, he learns that the girl's husband is dead, and the young man, whose name is Hareton Earnshaw, is not Heathcliff's son.

After supper, Lockwood is snowed in. Refused assistance home, he snatches a lantern from Joseph and is again attacked by dogs. Rescued by the housekeeper, Zillah, he is shown to a room.

COMMENT

Lockwood refers to the early hour at which dinner is served at Thrushcross Grange. His comment highlights the contrast between the remote world of the novel and the civilised world in which five o'clock was the fashionable time to dine.

Lockwood gets a lot of things wrong in this chapter. As readers, we realise the unreliability of his judgements about characters, and that we will have to make up our own minds about them.

Notice how the house, with its big fire, is warm and cheerful in physical terms, but the social atmosphere is strained and hostile.

Emily Brontë involves the reader in Lockwood's puzzlement and curiosity about the house and characters so that we want to read on.

References to the supernatural (e.g. words like 'devil' and 'fairy') prepare us for the next chapter.

Mrs Heathcliff's remark that she wouldn't be allowed to leave explains the chained gates and barred doors. We still wonder why she is a prisoner.

Hareton is discussed by Lockwood as a rustic 'clown' (p. 11). However, we see a hint of his natural generosity when he offers to take Lockwood home 'as far as the park' (p. 14).

GLOSSARY

Whet are ye for? ... tull him? What do you want? The master's down in the sheepfold. Go round by the end of the barn if you want to speak to him (Yorkshire **dialect** – see Literary Terms)

They's nobbut t'missis ... neeght There's only the mistress and she'll not open it even if you make your frightful noise until night

Nor-ne me! ... wi't Not me. I'll have nothing to do with it

discussed our meal ate our meal

Aw woonder hagh ... afore ye! I wonder how you can stand there in idleness and worse, when they've all gone out. But you're nothing, and it's no use talking – you'll never mend your evil ways; but go straight to the devil, like your mother before you

providential visitations the work of God

copestone final touch

smacked of King Lear were like the vengeful threats of Shakespeare's King Lear (*King Lear* II.4.274)

agait happening

wisht be quiet

CHAPTER 3

Lockwood's first encounter with names which arouse his curiosity and prove significant (see Structure).

Is your first reaction to Catherine and Heathcliff one of sympathy? If so, why?

In his room, Lockwood finds a box-bed, with sliding wood panels. Inside, he sees scratched on the window-sill the names: Catherine Earnshaw, Catherine Heathcliff and Catherine Linton.

He also discovers books, including a Bible containing the name 'Catherine Earnshaw'. In the margins of the books, is scrawled a diary telling how Catherine and Heathcliff had to listen to a sermon by Joseph. When they escaped afterwards onto the moors, they were punished. Lockwood falls asleep and dreams he is hearing a famous preacher. The dream ends with him being attacked by the congregation, and the preacher banging the pulpit. Waking, he realises the noise was a branch tapping the window.

Books appear frequently in the novel, and take on a symbolic significance (see Literary Terms and Language and Style). Find examples of what books mean to different characters.

In his second dream, Lockwood tries to stop the tree knocking by breaking the window. To his horror, his hand is grasped by icy fingers, and a voice, calling itself Catherine Linton, asks to be let in. Desperately, he rubs the wrist on the broken glass until it lets go, then piles books against the hole. As the voice continues, the pile of books begins to move. Lockwood wakes, shouting with fright.

Heathcliff enters and Lockwood describes his dream. Leaving the room, he overhears Heathcliff passionately appealing to Catherine. He passes the night downstairs, returning to the Grange next morning.

COMMENT

Notice that in his second dream, the civilised Lockwood is capable of violence and cruelty. Why do his actions seem so savage?

Lockwood feels secure in his box-bed against the turbulent world of Wuthering Heights. **Ironically** (see Literary Terms), he is attacked not from outside but by his own dreams.

Emily Brontë emphasises the closeness of Catherine and Heathcliff by such details as their sharing the cloak on their scamper on the moors (p. 19).

Lockwood tries to dismiss his nightmare but as the book continues, it is suggested that the ghost is not just his imagination.

Notice how Lockwood has difficulty finding his way home in the snow. He says he continually steered wrongly. This sums up his difficulties in judging characters and events in the last three chapters.

GLOSSARY

nut o'ered not over

lugs ears

laiking playing

scroop spine

riven torn

pawsed his fit kicked his feet

flaysome dreadful

owd Nick the Devil

Seventy Times Seven (Matthew 18: 21–22) Jesus's reply when asked if we should forgive sinners 'Til seven times?' means we should go on forgiving them no matter how many times they sin. However, Branderham uses Christ's words as an excuse for not forgiving people after their 490th sin!

changeling fairy child exchanged for a human

Grimalkin name for a cat

My human fixture and her satellites Nelly and the servants at the Grange

Test Yourself (Chapters 1–3)

Identify the speaker.

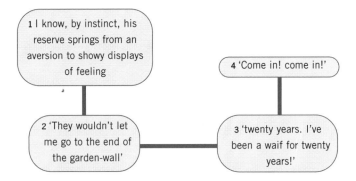

1 I know, by instinct, his reserve springs from an aversion to showy displays of feeling

4 'Come in! come in!'

2 'They wouldn't let me go to the end of the garden-wall'

3 'twenty years. I've been a waif for twenty years!'

Identify the person 'to whom' this comment refers.

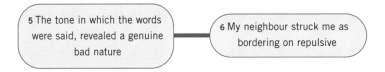

5 The tone in which the words were said, revealed a genuine bad nature

6 My neighbour struck me as bordering on repulsive

Check your answers on page 92.

Consider these issues.

a What is revealed of Lockwood as a character, and what Emily Brontë makes you think of him and his reliability as a **narrator** (see Literary Terms).

b Your opening impressions of the characters Lockwood meets.

c How the past is shown as alive and powerfully affecting the present.

d Differences and similarities between Heathcliff and Lockwood. Their names.

CHILDHOOD AND SEPARATION

CHAPTER 4

Heathcliff was a 'dirty, ragged, black-haired child' starving in the street (p. 32).

His curiosity aroused, Lockwood asks Mrs Dean, his housekeeper at Thrushcross Grange, to tell him about the family at Wuthering Heights. She tells him that Mrs Heathcliff is the daughter of her late master, Mr Linton. She also describes how Heathcliff was first brought to the Heights by her previous master, Mr Earnshaw, after a trip to Liverpool.

The outsider was resented by Earnshaw's wife and his two children, Hindley, aged fourteen, and Catherine, aged six. Mrs Dean admits how, as a young servant, she also mistreated the child. The child was christened Heathcliff, and Catherine and he became close friends. Mrs Dean eventually overcame her hostility to young Heathcliff, seeing how patiently he endured illness and Hindley's bullying.

COMMENT

Mrs Dean takes up the story in this chapter, becoming one of the main **narrators** (see Literary Terms) in the novel. Lockwood tells us what Mrs Dean told him. As in the case of Lockwood, Mrs Dean is not just a narrator. Her character, attitudes and ways of judging people make an important contribution to the novel (see Structure and Characters).

Notice how characters refer to Heathcliff as 'it'.

Note the contrasting ways in which Heathcliff is seen. Mr Earnshaw tells his wife she must take the child 'as a gift of God; though it's as dark almost as if it came from the devil' (p. 32). Hindley calls him an 'imp of Satan', whereas to Mrs Dean, after her change of heart, he is a 'lamb' (p. 34).

GLOSSARY

strike my colours surrender
indigenae local people
near miserly
a cuckoo's a cuckoo lays its egg in another bird's nest.
　　Heathcliff is compared to a baby cuckoo, growing larger than
　　other fledglings and pushing them out
dunnock sparrow

beaten tired out
fly up get angry
bairns children
thick friendly

CHAPTER 5

Catherine is described as mischievous and high-spirited, with 'a bold, saucy look' but with the 'sweetest smile' (p. 37).

In the period before Mr Earnshaw's death, Heathcliff becomes his favourite, causing resentment in Hindley. Hindley is sent to college, and old Earnshaw, influenced by the strict ideas of Joseph, becomes increasingly authoritarian, causing tension between him and Catherine. However, on Earnshaw's death, both she and Heathcliff are grief-stricken.

Running through the storm that accompanies the children's outburst of grief, Nelly fetched the Doctor. On her return she is struck by the innocence of the children as they comfort each other by imagining Earnshaw in heaven.

COMMENT

Emily Brontë portrays the character of Catherine Earnshaw, through the eyes of Mrs Dean, as having both unattractive and attractive qualities.

Look for other details that suggest the bond between them.

A number of details, like Heathcliff 'lying on the floor with his head in her lap' (p. 38), suggest the closeness of Heathcliff and Catherine.

GLOSSARY

pharisee hypocrite
frame hurry

CHAPTER 6

Hindley's degradation of Heathcliff shows his hatred for him.

Mrs Dean (Nelly) tells how Hindley returns, with a wife, for his father's funeral. He makes Heathcliff a labourer and denies him education.

Catherine and Heathcliff escape from Hindley's tyranny to the moors. One evening, Heathcliff returns alone and tells Nelly they have been to Thrushcross Grange and watched the Linton family through a window. The splendid world they saw fascinated them. However, in laughing at the spoilt Linton children, they were

CHILDHOOD AND SEPARATION

Compare the description of the furnishings (p. 42) with those of the Heights.

discovered and Catherine was seized by a bulldog. Inside, Edgar Linton recognised Catherine as the daughter of a neighbour. Heathcliff, however, was regarded as 'unfit for a decent house' (p. 45). Forced to leave without Catherine, he watched through the window, prepared to smash it if she had wanted to return. But she was happy being entertained as a young lady, and Heathcliff returned alone.

Mr Linton reprimands Hindley about his family's behaviour, and Heathcliff is told never to speak to Catherine again.

COMMENT

Heathcliff himself becomes a **narrator** (see Literary Terms) here, Nelly telling Lockwood what Heathcliff told her. His language, in his description of the dog (p. 44) and of his willingness to smash the window, is vivid and passionate, so we share his feelings (see Language and Style).

Heathcliff's love for Catherine is clearly shown, as well as his scorn for the Lintons.

Recall the example in Chapter 3.

The children first see the civilised luxury of the Grange, very different from the world they know, through a window. There are other examples in the novel of the use of windows to separate different worlds (see Language and Style).

Mr Linton is a landed gentleman and a magistrate, representing law and order. Notice that the respectable, civilised world of the Grange uses violence (the bulldog and threats of hanging) to protect its property.

GLOSSARY

these symptoms portended the symptoms indicated that Hindley's wife was developing tuberculosis. Emily herself, and three of her sisters, died of it

delf-case cupboard for crockery

Lascar East Indian sailor

negus wine and hot water

CHAPTER 7

Compare Nelly's description of Heathcliff's eyes as windows and 'devil's spies' (p. 51) with Lockwood's (Chapter 1). Look for other references to characters' eyes.

Heathcliff rejects Nelly's Christian moralising that 'we should learn to forgive'.

After five weeks at the Grange, Catherine returns finely dressed, very much a lady. Heathcliff has been treated as a servant in her absence, and, although she embraces him, her laughter at his uncouthness upsets him. On Christmas Day, the Linton children visit the Heights. Heathcliff's big effort to please Catherine by making himself 'decent' (p. 50) is scorned by Hindley.

When Edgar also makes fun of his appearance, Heathcliff throws hot sauce over him and is beaten by Hindley. Catherine is upset and later that evening climbs through the skylight into the room in which Heathcliff has been locked. Later, Heathcliff broods on how to 'pay Hindley back' (p. 55).

Here, Nelly breaks off her story, but Lockwood begs her to continue, praising her superior way of speaking. Nelly explains she has read a lot.

COMMENT

Emily Brontë suggests the beginnings of the conflict between Catherine's love for Heathcliff and her social ambition: 'She gazed concernedly at the dusky fingers she held in her own, and also at her dress' (p. 48).

Is this the origin of Heathcliff's plan of revenge?

Nelly suggests he might be a 'prince in disguise' (p. 51) with parents rich enough to buy both the Heights and the Grange.

Childhood and separation

Nelly sympathises with Heathcliff, reflecting sadly on 'the poor lad's situation' (p. 49). Heathcliff is a 'prisoner' in the garret (p. 54) but has also been imprisoned by Hindley in the degrading role of servant, which prevents him relating to Catherine on equal terms.

GLOSSARY   **beaver** fur hat

habit riding dress

cant bold

frame high notions of my birth imagine that I was nobly born

mess of victuals dish of food

CHAPTER 8   In June 1778, Hindley's wife, Frances, dies after giving birth to Hareton. Hindley falls into a life of drunken dissipation, victimising Heathcliff.

Nelly advances two years to 1780, describing how Catherine, now a local beauty of fifteen, is still strongly attached to Heathcliff, though she finds it hard to be friends with both him and Edgar. Heathcliff, aged sixteen, reduced to labouring by Hindley, has stopped trying to keep up with Catherine in his studies. She criticises his lack of intelligent conversation.

Catherine's 'ambition' is stressed by Nelly (p. 60).

How does the chapter show Catherine's 'headstrong' side (p. 59)?

One day, in Hindley's absence, Catherine invites Edgar to call, but Heathcliff remains behind. He leaves on Edgar's arrival, but the tension in the following scene leads to Catherine pinching Nelly, and slapping Edgar. Edgar tries to leave, but Catherine stops him, and they finally declare themselves lovers.

COMMENT   Catherine finds it increasingly difficult to reconcile her feelings for both Heathcliff and Edgar. When Heathcliff asks if anybody is coming that afternoon, she lies: 'Not that I know of' (p. 62). We also see the violent side to Catherine.

The chapter contains examples of **imagery** (see Literary Terms). Nelly describes Heathcliff and Edgar using images of different landscapes (p. 63). Notice also the use of animal imagery, both here, in relation to Edgar and Catherine (p. 66), and elsewhere (see Style).

GLOSSARY   **consumption** tuberculosis, a disease of the lungs
                      rush of a lass frail girl
                      wanted spirit lacked vitality
                      fowling-piece shotgun

CHAPTER 9

Hindley, drunk, drops Hareton over the bannister but Heathcliff catches the child accidentally.

Catherine tells Nelly she has agreed to marry Edgar. She admits part of her feels this is wrong, describing a dream in which she was thrown out of heaven onto the heath at Wuthering Heights and woke 'sobbing for joy' (p. 73). She claims that as Hindley has reduced Heathcliff to an uneducated labourer, it would degrade her to marry him. Just then, Heathcliff, who has been listening, unseen by Catherine, leaves. He doesn't hear her go on to describe her love for him (see Themes).

Think what Catherine's dream is telling her. Remember the 'heaven' seen through the Linton's window by Catherine and Heathcliff (p. 42).

Too late, Nelly reveals that Heathcliff overheard the conversation. Catherine, distraught, searches for him in a violent thunderstorm. Developing a fever, she convalesces at Thrushcross Grange, where the Linton parents become infected and die. On her return home, nothing has been heard of Heathcliff and after three years she marries Edgar.

COMMENT

Heathcliff's desire for revenge (see Themes) on Hindley shows in his regret at having saved Hareton's life.

Nelly criticises Catherine's reasons for marrying Edgar. Her social ambition can be seen in her explanation that Edgar 'will be rich, and I shall like to be the greatest woman of the neighbourhood' (p. 71).

CHILDHOOD AND SEPARATION

As we see later on, Edgar finds it impossible to feel as Catherine wants.

Catherine sees no reason why marrying Edgar should affect her relationship with Heathcliff. Her selfish expectation that others' feelings will fit in with her desires is shown in her description of how Edgar should behave to Heathcliff: 'He must shake off his antipathy, and tolerate him' (p. 74). Catherine is also wrong in assuming Heathcliff 'comprehends' her feelings for Edgar (p. 75).

Note Catherine's association of the image of 'fire' with herself and Heathcliff, and 'frost' with Edgar (p. 73).

Natural **imagery** (see Literary Terms) is used in Catherine's description of her feelings for Heathcliff and Edgar (see Language and Style). Her love for Edgar is subject to change whereas her love for Heathcliff 'resembles the eternal rocks beneath' (p. 75).

GLOSSARY

the bairnies grat the children cried

The mither beneath the mools the mother under the earth (buried)

Milo Greek athlete eaten by wolves. A similar fate would befall anyone coming between Catherine and Heathcliff

nowt nobody

girt eedle seeght great idle sight

war un war worse and worse

plottered blundered

Hahsomdiver however

offald craters worthless creatures

Noah and Lot Biblical figures spared by God because of their goodness

Jonah a person who brings bad luck

Aw's niver wonder I shouldn't be surprised

them as is chozzen those who are chosen by God for salvation

gentle or simple upper or lower class

bolt intuh th' hahs rush into the house

A Identify the speaker.

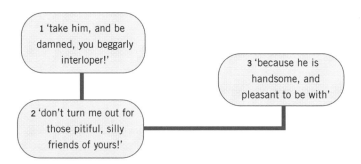

1 'take him, and be damned, you beggarly interloper!'

2 'don't turn me out for those pitiful, silly friends of yours!'

3 'because he is handsome, and pleasant to be with'

Identify the person 'to whom' this comment refers.

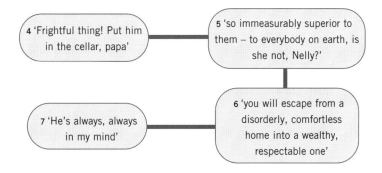

4 'Frightful thing! Put him in the cellar, papa'

5 'so immeasurably superior to them – to everybody on earth, is she not, Nelly?'

7 'He's always, always in my mind'

6 'you will escape from a disorderly, comfortless home into a wealthy, respectable one'

Check your answers on page 92.

B Consider these issues.

a How Emily Brontë develops the relationship between Catherine and Heathcliff.

b The portrayal of the contrasting worlds of Wuthering Heights and Thrushcross Grange.

c The developing conflict between Catherine's feelings for Edgar and for Heathcliff.

d How Emily Brontë shows the hatred between Heathcliff and Hindley.

THE RETURN OF HEATHCLIFF

CHAPTER 10

Over three years later, and after Catherine and Edgar have been married six months, Heathcliff returns. Edgar is surprised to see the 'ploughboy' changed into 'a tall, athletic, well-formed man' showing no signs of 'former degradation' (pp. 87–8). He resents Catherine's joy in the reunion.

Nelly also notices a 'half-civilized ferocity' lurking in 'eyes full of black fire'.

Isabella, now eighteen, becomes infatuated with Heathcliff, accusing Catherine of selfishly keeping him to herself. In retaliation, Catherine reveals Isabella's feelings in front of Heathcliff, who despises Isabella but is interested that she would inherit Edgar's property.

COMMENT

A sense of mystery surrounds where Heathcliff has been and the source of his money. Perhaps he has been to university, fought in the American War of Independence or been a highwayman.

Recall Nelly's fantasies about his birth in Chapter 7.

Nelly plays a role here, carrying Heathcliff's message to Catherine. Her loyalty to Edgar is shown when she tells him of Heathcliff's arrival. She explains: 'My heart invariably cleaved to the master's, in preference to Catherine's side' (p. 99).

A sense of tension and foreboding is developed. Nelly says of Catherine and Edgar's marriage: 'for the space of half a year, the gunpowder lay as harmless as sand, because no fire came near to explode it' (p. 84).

Notice other details (see the end of the chapter) contributing to this ominous atmosphere

Catherine assumes, as in Chapter 9, that Edgar should feel as *she* wishes and 'must get accustomed' to Heathcliff (p. 90). Consider whether Edgar's feelings are understandable in the circumstances.

Nelly believes Catherine and Edgar were 'in possession of a deep and growing happiness' (p. 84). However,

Catherine herself says of the period of Heathcliff's absence: 'Oh, I've endured very, very bitter misery' (p. 91). We may question the reliability of Nelly's view.

GLOSSARY   **sizar** poor student with a university grant

sough ditch

in default of heirs male in the absence of male heirs

dog in the manger person who stops others having what they themselves don't want

we's hae a Crahnr's 'quest ... grand 'sizes we shall have a coroner's inquest soon at our house. One of them almost got his finger cut off stopping the other killing himself like a calf. That's the master, you know, who's so set on going to the Grand Assizes (Heaven)

girn snarl

t' fooil gangs banning ... cham'er the fool (Hindley) goes cursing and raving to his room

carn cahnt his brass can count his money

t' Broad Road the road to ruin

t' pikes the gates

CHAPTER 11

At the Heights, Nelly meets young Hareton who throws a stone at her. Heathcliff has taught him to swear at his father. When Heathcliff appears, Nelly runs away.

When Heathcliff next visits the Grange, Nelly sees him embracing Isabella. When Catherine is angry with him, he accuses her of treating him 'infernally' (p. 103) and expresses his determination to get revenge. Nelly then tells Edgar what has happened, and in the ensuing quarrel Catherine locks the door so Edgar must face Heathcliff alone. Humiliated by Heathcliff, Edgar strikes him and leaves by another door. Heathcliff escapes and Catherine tells Nelly she means to break both men's hearts by breaking her own.

THE RETURN OF HEATHCLIFF

Do you think, as Nelly does, that Catherine should control her passionate temper in this scene?

When Edgar asks her to decide between Heathcliff or himself, Catherine flies into a frenzy, locks herself away and refuses food. Edgar warns Isabella that if she encourages Heathcliff's attentions, he will disown her.

COMMENT

The change in young Hareton relates to the theme of Heathcliff's revenge. Just as Hindley 'degraded' young Heathcliff so that Catherine chose not to marry him, now Heathcliff ensures Hindley's son, Hareton, grows up brutalised.

Heathcliff speaks in passionate and extreme language of the pain he has suffered at Catherine's hands as if she is a 'tyrant' inflicting 'torture' on him (p. 104).

Compare this description with Catherine's reference to 'frost' and 'fire' on p. 73.

Catherine says Edgar's veins are 'full of ice-water' but hers are 'boiling' (p. 109).

Nelly is loyal to Edgar and disapproves of Catherine. It is when Catherine overhears Nelly reporting to Edgar that her 'fit of frenzy' (p. 110) was put on, that she rushes to her room.

GLOSSARY

sand-pillar milestone

elf-locked with tangled hair

Judas Judas Iscariot, the disciple who betrayed Jesus

levelled my palace destroyed my happiness (by marrying Edgar)

sucking leveret a person lacking in spirit (literally a young hare)

CHAPTER 12

Catherine refuses food for three days, and Edgar shuts himself up with his books. Nelly judges that Catherine is acting, so doesn't tell Edgar about her condition. Catherine becomes delirious. She asks Nelly to open the window and is carried away by memories of her childhood, imagining she is back at the Heights in the room with the oak-panelled bed, which she shared with Heathcliff.

This is the room of Lockwood's nightmare (Chapter 3). The detail of the black press (p. 114) recalls the clothes-press (p. 16).

She feels great grief and despair that she doesn't at first understand. She then links it with her separation from Heathcliff and being 'wrenched' from the Heights to be 'the lady of Thrushcross Grange, and the wife of a stranger' (p. 116). In her fever, she imagines seeing the lights of the Heights. When Edgar sees how ill Catherine is, he is angry with Nelly for not telling him. But Catherine rejects him, blaming Nelly for being her enemy.

Remember how Catherine's dream revealed her true feelings to her in Chapter 9.

On her way to fetch the doctor, Nelly rescues Isabella's dog which has been hung outside. She hears of Isabella's elopement with Heathcliff, but decides not to burden Edgar with it. Next morning Isabella's absence is discovered and Edgar disowns her.

COMMENT

Nelly plays an active role in withholding and passing on information. Looking back, she admits she was wrong to distort the facts in telling Catherine about Edgar's involvement with his books: 'I should not have spoken so, if I had known her true condition' (p. 111).

This chapter is important, showing Catherine's painful realisation of her true situation. However,

THE RETURN OF HEATHCLIFF

Nelly's judgement of Catherine's state of mind is limited: all she can say is: 'She has been talking nonsense' (p. 118). This makes us feel more sympathetic to Catherine.

How do you respond to her concern for the lapwings' nest 'full of little skeletons' (p. 113)?

Some find Catherine's behaviour (e.g. tearing the pillow with her teeth) so grotesque and undignified as to lessen their sympathy for her. But remember we see Catherine through Nelly's eyes. Nelly herself admits she was overconfident in her own judgement that she was the 'one sensible soul at the Grange' (p. 111).

GLOSSARY   **pigeons' feathers** according to Yorkshire folklore, the soul could not leave the body of a dying person lying on a bed containing pigeons' feathers

elf-bolts arrowheads shot by fairies

CHAPTER 13

Catherine is ill for two months with 'brain fever'. Nursed by Edgar, she recovers in the spring, but is still weak, foretelling her own death. She is expecting a child.

Consider the effect of the use of Yorkshire dialect by Hareton and Joseph in creating a world alien to Isabella.

Nelly then reads a letter she received from Isabella. Realising her marriage was a mistake, Isabella wonders if Heathcliff is a man or a devil. She describes the hostility she met at the Heights. When she tried to befriend young Hareton, he threatened to set a dog on her. She describes meeting Hindley who glared 'like a hungry wolf' (p. 128), and showed her a fascinating weapon. He was afraid he might kill Heathcliff before he had recovered money lost at gambling.

Why do you think Heathcliff swears at her when she refers to 'our' room?

No room was prepared for her, and Heathcliff's was locked, so she spent the night downstairs. The letter ends begging Nelly to visit her.

COMMENT   Through Isabella's eyes, we get another way of looking
                   at characters and events.

Emily Brontë   Isabella had been attracted to Heathcliff, but once at
provides yet   the Heights she yearns to return to 'my delightful
another narrator   house, containing the only people I loved on earth'
as Isabella takes (p. 129). In this respect, she can be compared to
over the story.   Catherine, who had been attracted to the world of
                   Thrushcross Grange, but then yearned for the Heights
                   (Chapter 12).

GLOSSARY   **Mim! mim! mim!** Prim. Joseph is mocking Isabella's way of
                     speaking
                   ortherings orders
                   thible wooden spoon
                   nave fist
                   pale t' guilp off skim the milk off
                   deaved aht knocked out
                   meeterly sufficiently
                   mells ont meddles with it
                   madling fool
                   pining starving
                   plisky temper
                   Him as allas maks a third the Devil

CHAPTER 14

Nelly tells Edgar of Isabella's return but he refuses to
write to her. Nelly calls at the Heights to find Isabella
looking neglected, but Heathcliff looking quite the
gentleman.

Hearing of Catherine's illness, Heathcliff insists on
seeing her. Nelly objects as this would hinder
Catherine's recovery and she tries to deter him by
saying that Catherine has nearly forgotten him.
Heathcliff denies this and is dismissive about Edgar.
Isabella is clearly a prisoner, and when Nelly protests at

THE RETURN OF HEATHCLIFF

How justified is Heathcliff's demands for an interview with Catherine,
Heathcliff's he threatens to imprison her too. As Heathcliff
comment that threatens to fight his way to Catherine, Nelly
Edgar is 'scarcely a reluctantly agrees to arrange a meeting.
degree dearer to her
than her dog'. Dr Kenneth arrives to see Lockwood and Nelly breaks
off her story.

COMMENT   Isabella describes Heathcliff as 'a lying fiend! a monster,
and not a human being!' (p. 140). Consider what he
actually does to justify this comment.

Note the gruesome Heathcliff's mistreatment of Isabella is part of his
metaphor (see revenge against Edgar.
Literary Terms) in
which the pitiless Lockwood, who fled from emotional commitment,
Heathcliff likens his rather ridiculously associates himself with Heathcliff by
victims to 'worms' resolving to avoid involvement with Catherine's
(p. 141). daughter in case she turns out like her mother. This
emphasises, by contrast, the extreme nature of
Heathcliff's passion.

GLOSSARY   **labour of Hercules** a difficult task
brach bitch
dree sad

CHAPTER 15

Nelly gives Heathcliff's letter to Catherine when Edgar
is at church. Heathcliff doesn't wait for her answer.
Finding the house open, he bursts in and takes her in
Notice the animal his arms.
image of the mad
dog Nelly uses to He sees she is going to die and in a scene of passionate
describe Heathcliff's recrimination Catherine accuses Heathcliff of killing
violent passion (see her and he accuses her of breaking both their hearts by
Language and marrying Edgar: '*Why* did you betray your own heart …
Style). You have killed yourself' (p. 149). The quarrel ends
with them weeping in each other's arms. When Edgar

enters, Catherine is unconscious. Placing her body in Edgar's arms, Heathcliff goes outside.

COMMENT   Nelly says Catherine's gaze seems fixed beyond objects around her, and after Heathcliff's arrival Catherine describes her body as a prison in which she is 'tired of being enclosed' (p. 148). The desire to escape from this world is also a theme in Emily Brontë's poetry (see Themes and Broader Perspectives).

Recall Catherine's   Heathcliff mentions the 'torture' Catherine is
description of their   inflicting on him; she retorts: 'Why shouldn't you
love as 'a source of   suffer? I do!' (p. 147). This shows their love's
little visible   destructive side.
delight' (p. 75).

Heathcliff accuses Catherine of betraying her deepest feelings by marrying Edgar when she really loved Heathcliff. Consider the justice of her answer: 'You left me too' (p. 149).

CHAPTER 16

That night, Catherine dies after giving birth to a daughter. Heathcliff, outside in the garden, realises Catherine is dead before Nelly tells him. She pities his anguish. His response is to hope Catherine will 'wake in torment' (p. 155) and haunt him.

Another example of   Later, Heathcliff enters unobserved through a
a window image   window and replaces a lock of Edgar's hair from
(see Language and   Catherine's locket with a lock of his own. Nelly
Style).   retrieves Edgar's hair and encloses both locks twisted together.

COMMENT   The fact that Edgar has no son suits Heathcliff's revenge. Old Mr Linton left his estate to Edgar, but if Edgar has no sons, the estate passes to Isabella. As she is married to Heathcliff, her property would become his.

THE RETURN OF HEATHCLIFF

Heathcliff's appeal that Catherine haunt him foreshadows later chapters (and recalls Chapter 3).

The distraught Heathcliff imagines himself talking to Catherine. His claim, 'I *cannot* live without my life!' (p. 155) recalls Catherine's 'Nelly, I *am* Heathcliff!' (p. 75).

Catherine is buried in a corner of the churchyard 'where the wall is so low that heath and bilberry plants have climbed over it from the moor' (p. 156). This is apt, bearing in mind Catherine's love of the moors. It also shows the effects of time and change which pervade the whole novel.

CHAPTER 17

The day after Catherine's funeral, Isabella arrives at the Grange. She describes how the previous evening, when Heathcliff returned, Hindley locked the doors, intending to kill him. Despite Isabella's hatred for Heathcliff, she shrunk from murder and warned him. He grabbed Hindley's weapon through the window, wounding him and forcing an entry. According to Isabella, he then trampled on Hindley's unconscious body.

Isabella's fascination with the weapon is shown in her letter (p. 130).

Next morning, Isabella taunted the grieving Heathcliff, and he threw a knife which wounded her. In the ensuing struggle between him and Hindley, Isabella escaped. Her story ends, and Nelly describes how, a few months later, having fled to the South, she has a son, Linton.

How might Isabella's reference to seeing Catherine's eyes in Hindley (p. 168) affect Heathcliff? (Remember his words to Catherine about her eyes on p. 149.)

Six months after Catherine's death, Hindley dies; Joseph suspects Heathcliff. Edgar tries to take Hareton, his nephew, away from Heathcliff, but relents when Heathcliff threatens to retaliate by taking his own son, Linton, away from Isabella. As a result of Hindley's debts, Heathcliff now owns Wuthering Heights and Hareton lives there as a servant.

COMMENT   The weather sets the mood for Catherine's death and
           funeral: 'the primroses and crocuses were hidden under
           wintry drifts' (p. 156) (see Language and Style).

           Isabella sees Heathcliff as a monster 'not a human
           being' (p. 159) and her description of his attack on
           Hindley shows him in a savagely brutal light. We get a
           different version of this incident from Heathcliff, in
           Chapter 29.

Isabella's use of   The revenge theme is developed (see Themes). Isabella
'degrading'   adopts Heathcliff's morality of revenge, and, in hurting
(p. 168), is   him verbally, enjoys 'the delight of paying wrong for
particularly   wrong' (p. 166). Heathcliff himself, now that he owns
wounding.   Wuthering Heights, chillingly plans revenge on
Catherine earlier   Hindley for his own upbringing by treating Hindley's
said marrying   son, Hareton, in the same way: 'Now, my bonny lad,
Heathcliff would   you are mine! And we'll see if one tree won't grow as
'degrade' her   crooked as another' (p. 173). Hareton's hanging of the
(p. 73).   puppies shows Heathcliff's influence.

GLOSSARY   **black father** the Devil
            basilisk a mythical serpent whose gaze could kill
            an eye for an eye revenge, in the manner of the Old Testament
              (Exodus 21:24)
            clouded windows of hell Heathcliff's eyes
            delivered another another sentence. Isabella hopes her words
              cut as deeply as Heathcliff's knife
            taen tent taken care

A *Identify the speaker.*

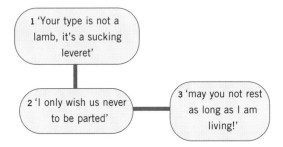

1 'Your type is not a lamb, it's a sucking leveret'

2 'I only wish us never to be parted'

3 'may you not rest as long as I am living!'

Identify the person 'to whom' this comment refers.

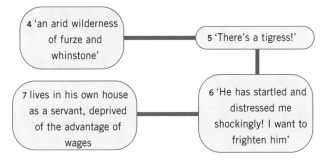

4 'an arid wilderness of furze and whinstone'

5 'There's a tigress!'

7 lives in his own house as a servant, deprived of the advantage of wages

6 'He has startled and distressed me shockingly! I want to frighten him'

Check your answers on page 92.

B *Consider these issues.*

a Your response to Catherine in this section. Whether you feel that she retains enough of your sympathy to become a pitiful and **tragic** (see Literary Terms) figure.

b The presentation of Heathcliff. Whether you agree that Isabella's description of him as a sub-human 'monster' sums him up adequately.

c Your impressions of Edgar. Whether he is a 'milk-blooded coward' (p. 107).

d Whether Isabella, despite her genteel background, also shows a potential for violence beneath the surface of her 'dainty elegance' (p. 90).

e The role played by Nelly, and how her words and actions affect events.

CHAPTER 18

The story moves forward twelve years to June 1797. Catherine's daughter, Cathy, has her mother's high spirits but, unlike her mother, 'her anger was never furious; her love never fierce: it was deep and tender' (p. 174).

Why do you think Cathy has not been allowed outside the park of Thrushcross Grange by herself?

Edgar hears from Isabella that she is dying and goes to see her. Cathy, now thirteen, escapes from the park on her pony. Nelly discovers her at the Heights. Heathcliff is not there, but she has met Hareton who has shown her Penistone Crags. In her ignorance, she takes Hareton for a servant and is horrified to learn he is her cousin. When she and Nelly return home, Nelly persuades her not to tell Edgar of the visit.

COMMENT

The story of the second generation of Earnshaws and Lintons now begins.

Cathy has inherited physical features from both her mother and father. Consider whether you agree that her character shows the good qualities of both the Earnshaws and the Lintons.

Cathy assumes Hareton is a servant because of his speech, dress and manner. We see the results of Heathcliff's treating him like a labourer.

GLOSSARY

fairishes fairies
offald awful
near mean

CHAPTERS 19–20

Isabella dies and Edgar returns with her son, Linton Heathcliff. Cathy welcomes him, but the sickly Linton responds like a baby. That evening Joseph brings a demand from Heathcliff that Linton return to the Heights with him. Edgar reluctantly promises to send him the next day.

THE SECOND GENERATION

Next morning, when Nelly takes Linton to the Heights, Heathcliff mockingly calls him a 'puling chicken', and his mother 'a wicked slut' (p. 192). However, he assures Nelly he will educate Linton as a 'gentleman' as he wants the triumph of seeing his descendant inherit the Grange. Linton is upset when Nelly leaves.

COMMENT Linton is a delicate, effeminate boy physically similar to Edgar and Isabella. However, Nelly says he has a 'sickly peevishness' (p. 185) that Edgar lacks, and has not the 'sparkling spirit' (p. 190) of which Isabella was capable.

Linton contributes to Heathcliff's plan of revenge. When Edgar dies, Linton will inherit the Grange, and if Linton died young, Heathcliff would be his successor.

GLOSSARY *Chapter 19*
Aw munn't goa back 'baht him I mustn't go back without him
Hathecliff maks noa 'cahnt uh t'mother, nur yah norther Heathcliff takes no account of the mother, nor of you either

Chapter 20
brown study day dream
cipher nonentity (insulting reference to Edgar)
Is there owt ails th'victuals? Is there anything wrong with the food?

CHAPTER 21

On March 20 1800, the anniversary of her birth and her mother's death, Cathy persuades Nelly to take her on the moors. They meet Heathcliff who lures them to Wuthering Heights, revealing his plan that Cathy and Linton should marry.

Linton dislikes open windows and 'must have a fire in the middle of summer' (p. 195).

Cathy meets the feeble Linton. Hareton, whom Heathcliff confesses he could have loved if he had not been Hindley's son, is tongue-tied before Cathy and cannot even read his own name over the door. Heathcliff reveals his pleasure in seeing Hareton suffer in the 'coarseness and ignorance' (p. 202) to which he himself was reduced by Hindley.

After Cathy's return home, she writes secretly to Linton. Nelly finds Linton's love letters and suspects Heathcliff's involvement. She burns them, threatening to tell Edgar unless Cathy stops communicating with Linton.

COMMENT

Heathcliff knows about the laws of inheritance. If Edgar died, his property would go to Linton (and therefore Heathcliff), but he wants Linton to marry Catherine to strengthen his claim.

Linton Heathcliff is physically weak, claiming a four mile walk to the Grange would kill him, and he spitefully mocks the illiterate Hareton's 'frightful Yorkshire pronunciation' (p. 204).

Which earlier scenes show Heathcliff feeling similar humiliation to Hareton's?

The way Hareton is taunted by Linton, and humiliated in front of Cathy, recalls Edgar's mockery of Heathcliff in Chapter 7. However, Linton's mockery of Hareton is more deliberate than Edgar's. Hareton's reaction is also different: he restrains his anger whereas Heathcliff threw sauce at Edgar.

Heathcliff's pursuit of revenge on Hindley by making Hareton grow up an ignorant oaf, is particularly callous. He even says he can sympathise with Hareton's feelings of frustration 'having felt them myself' (p. 202).

Heathcliff believes Hareton is imprisoned in the degradation he himself suffered: 'I've got him faster than his scoundrel of a father secured me' (p. 202). However, he is wrong in gloating that Hareton 'had first-rate qualities, and they are lost'. Hareton later escapes the prison of his ignorance through his relationship with Cathy.

GLOSSARY

extra-animal not animal; cultivated or refined

one is gold put to the use of paving stones one (Hareton) has good qualities which are misused

The other is tin the other (Linton) is like worthless metal masquerading as something valuable

lath weakling

CHAPTERS *22–23*

That autumn, Edgar falls ill. Walking in the park with Nelly, Cathy is sad that one day her father and Nelly will die. Nelly reassures her that Edgar may live a long time if she doesn't upset him by continuing her relationship with Linton.

Heathcliff plays on Cathy's pity for Linton and her conscience.

Climbing on the park wall, Cathy drops her hat, and, in retrieving it, finds herself the other side of a locked door. Before Nelly can get the key, Heathcliff rides by. He tells Cathy that Linton is dying and only she can save him. This worries Cathy and next day she and Nelly go to the Heights.

Linton's spitefulness shows in his enjoyment of Cathy's distress.

On Cathy's arrival, Linton behaves selfishly and childishly. During a quarrel, Cathy is upset by his insisting that her mother hated her father, and pushes his chair, which makes him cough. Linton exaggerates his suffering, frightening Cathy so that she promises to come again.

Nelly is ill for three weeks. Cathy cares for her, but secretly visits Linton.

COMMENT

Vivid physical details are used to describe the natural surroundings and weather (see Language and Style). Nelly describes 'a fresh watery afternoon, when the turf

Explore how natural description is used in this chapter.

and paths were rustling with moist, withered leaves, and the cold blue sky was half hidden by clouds' (p. 212). These and other details create **atmosphere** (see Literary Terms) and help convey the characters' feelings.

Cathy is caught in a conflict. She loves her father, but her conscience and compassion lead her to disobey him.

Linton is obsessed with his own physical comforts and emotionally blackmails Cathy: 'You ought to come because you have hurt me' (p. 223). This is more like a mother and child relationship than one between lovers.

GLOSSARY

Chapter 22
starved and sackless cold and depressed
canty cheerful
Slough of Despond a state of despair (in Bunyan's *The Pilgrim's Progress*)

Chapter 23
elysium heaven
pathos a quality that arouses pity

CHAPTER 24

How do the descriptions show the contrasting characters of Cathy and Linton (pp. 228–9)?

Cathy tells Nelly about her secret visits. Once, she and Linton nearly quarrelled over the best way to spend a July day. Another time, when Hareton wanted to show he could read his name over the door, she called him a 'dunce'. Later, as Cathy was about to read to Linton, Hareton angrily forced them into the kitchen. Linton flew into a rage and started coughing blood.

What do you think Hareton might be trying to say?

When Cathy finally set off for home, she was stopped by Hareton. Fearing he might murder her, she 'gave him a cut' with her whip (p. 232) and galloped home. On her next visit, Linton blamed her for the incident, although on a later occasion he repented of his behaviour and she forgave him. Cathy says she has learnt to 'endure' Linton's 'selfishness and spite' (p. 234). When Nelly tells Edgar of the visits, he forbids them.

COMMENT

Books represent the educated, civilised world that Cathy and Linton share but from which Hareton, an illiterate labourer, is excluded.

Consider the significance of Hareton being able to read his name over the door.

Cathy's judgement that Hareton is a fool who thought himself as clever as Linton 'because he could spell his own name' (p. 230) is unfair. Nelly points out he was 'intelligent as a child' and we can see that he is ashamed of his failings. Cathy is one of many characters who misjudge others.

Hearing Linton shriek that he will kill Hareton, Joseph says: 'That's father!' (p. 232), suggesting that he has inherited, if on a pathetic scale, some of Heathcliff's qualities.

GLOSSARY

Aw wer sure he'd sarve ye eht I was sure he'd teach you a lesson
skift shift
uh orther side of either side (from each parent)
bahn going

CHAPTERS 25–26

Nelly tells Lockwood that these events happened just over a year a year before (in winter 1800). She wonders whether a relationship might develop between him and Cathy, but he feels it might disturb his 'tranquillity' (p. 236).

How do Edgar's feelings towards the first Catherine affect his thoughts about death?

Nelly continues her story, describing Edgar's declining health and approaching death. Believing that a marriage with Linton (the heir to the Grange) is the only way of providing for Cathy, he reluctantly agrees to their meeting on the moors under Nelly's guardianship.

That summer, Nelly and Cathy meet Linton. As he doesn't seem to enjoy Cathy's company, she suggests going, but Linton begs her not to leave as he fears Heathcliff's anger. Cathy stays for half an hour, most of which Linton spends asleep, then goes, promising to return.

COMMENT   Edgar had agreed that Cathy and Linton could meet near the Grange. However, Linton is not at the agreed meeting-place, and Catherine and Nelly are led by a herd-boy closer to the Heights before they find him. Heathcliff is luring them away from the safety of the Grange.

Does Linton seem to have changed since his previous appearance?

When Cathy sees Linton lying on the heather, it reminds her of his ideal way of spending a July day (in Chapter 24). **Ironically** (see Literary Terms), in view of Linton's situation and the pervading sense of Heathcliff's influence, she adds: 'only there are clouds' (p. 240).

CHAPTER 27

Edgar is dying, but Cathy goes with Nelly to meet Linton, as she promised. He has a secret that he dare not reveal and is terrified he will be killed if Cathy leaves him. Heathcliff appears and persuades Cathy and Nelly to help Linton back to the Heights. Once there, he imprisons them. Cathy struggles with Heathcliff for the key to the door, but he beats her.

Do you think Cathy should have refused to go to the Heights?

Whilst Heathcliff goes for the horses, Linton tells Cathy that his father wants them to get married next day. On Heathcliff's return, Cathy promises to marry Linton if she is allowed home, as her absence will upset her father. Heathcliff says he will enjoy Edgar's misery, refusing to release her until after the marriage. Next morning, Heathcliff takes Cathy away.

COMMENT

Cathy's struggle with Heathcliff for the key (p. 249) recalls the struggle between her mother and Edgar in Chapter 11.

Cathy is reluctant to disobey her dying father and go to the Heights, but Heathcliff uses Linton as a decoy, exploiting Cathy's loyalty and compassion. The spirited way she stands up to Heathcliff, 'her black eyes flashing with passion' (p. 248) recalls her mother.

We see more of Linton's selfishness. All he can say after Heathcliff beats Cathy is: 'you are letting your tears fall into my cup! I won't drink that' (p. 250). His enjoyment of others' pain is suggested by Heathcliff's claim that Linton will 'torture any number of cats if their teeth be drawn' (p. 253).

GLOSSARY

ling heather

Lees grazing land

spleen bad temper

cockatrice mythical monster with a cock's head and dragon's tail

eft lizard

CHAPTER 28

On the fifth day, Zillah, the housekeeper, releases Nelly. Linton tells her that Cathy is still a prisoner, and that now they are married all her property, including her books, is his. He describes how he tried to take a

Do you have any sympathy with Linton in this chapter?

locket from her containing pictures of her parents, and how Heathcliff struck her and crushed Edgar's portrait.

Nelly returns home, where the dying Edgar tries to change his will to protect Cathy's fortune from Heathcliff. However, Heathcliff has bribed the lawyer who delays until too late. Cathy escapes from the Heights and is with her father when he dies. However, the Grange is now under Heathcliff's control.

COMMENT

Linton is unable to sympathise with Cathy as she sympathised with him.

Linton describes Heathcliff's brutality to Cathy vividly: 'she … showed me her cheek cut on the inside, against her teeth, and her mouth filling with blood' (p. 258). This kind of scene led some contemporary critics to condemn the book for its violence.

Why does Mr Green, the lawyer, try to stop Edgar being buried beside his wife?

Cathy escapes through the window in her mother's room. This and the fir tree she climbs down figure in Lockwood's dream (Chapter 3).

Edgar dies convinced of reunion with Catherine. As he tells Cathy: 'I am going to her; and you darling child shall come to us' (p. 261).

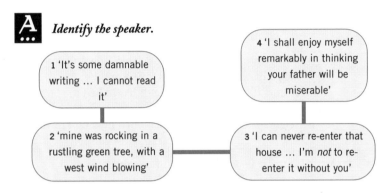

A *Identify the speaker.*

1 'It's some damnable writing ... I cannot read it'

4 'I shall enjoy myself remarkably in thinking your father will be miserable'

2 'mine was rocking in a rustling green tree, with a west wind blowing'

3 'I can never re-enter that house ... I'm *not* to re-enter it without you'

Identify the person 'to whom' this comment refers.

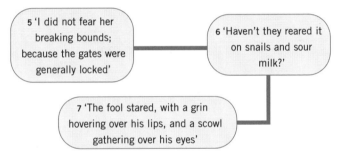

5 'I did not fear her breaking bounds; because the gates were generally locked'

6 'Haven't they reared it on snails and sour milk?'

7 'The fool stared, with a grin hovering over his lips, and a scowl gathering over his eyes'

Check your answers on page 92.

B *Consider these issues.*

a Your response to Cathy, how she is like and unlike her mother and father.

b The kind of love relationship Cathy has with Linton.

c Whether Linton embodies the worst qualities of his parents, and whether you care about Heathcliff's mistreatment of him.

d The similarities between Hareton and Heathcliff when young, particularly in the way their degradation affects their relationships with the two Catherines.

e Whether Heathcliff's rejection by Catherine in Chapter 9 explains and justifies his relentless revenge.

f The part played by references to walls, windows, doors and keys in emphasising the themes of imprisonment and escape.

CHAPTER *29*

What do you think of Cathy's insight into the reasons for Heathcliff's cruelty?

The day after Edgar's funeral, Heathcliff fetches Cathy, saying Linton has been punished for helping her escape and hates her. She asserts her power to love and forgive Linton despite his bad nature, attributing Heathcliff's cruelty to his misery and lack of anyone to love him.

Heathcliff tells Nelly that the previous day he had Catherine's coffin uncovered and removed the lid. Her face was still recognisable. He removed one side of her coffin, arranging for this to be done to his own coffin after his death, to allow their reunion. He describes how, after Catherine's funeral, he also uncovered her coffin. About to break in, he suddenly sensed her presence near him, and followed her eagerly back to the Heights. However, the doors were locked by Hindley

Remember Heathcliff's plea to Catherine to haunt him in Chapter 16 (p. 155).

and Isabella. In desperation, he broke in and rushed upstairs, but, although he felt Catherine's presence, she didn't appear. Since then, being haunted by this sense of her presence has been 'torture' (p. 266).

Heathcliff finishes his story, taking Cathy to the Heights.

COMMENT

Cathy stands up to Heathcliff courageously. She believes in love and forgiveness.

Emily Brontë uses Heathcliff as narrator (see Literary Terms) for the second time. His use of language allows us to share directly his physical sensations as he describes Catherine's 'warm breath …displacing the sleet-laden wind' (p. 266). We see things from Heathcliff's point of view and understand his feelings. In Chapter 17, Isabella portrayed his violent treatment of Hindley as sustained sadism (p. 164). Here we see the same scene through

AN END AND A BEGINNING

Consider how you react to Heathcliff after this chapter. Despite his behaviour in preceding chapters, do you have some sympathy for him?

Heathcliff's eyes: he was so desperate to see Catherine that he hardly noticed Hindley: 'I remember stopping to kick the breath out of him, and then hurrying upstairs' (p. 266).

Nelly's description of the 'painful appearance of mental tension' on Heathcliff's face (p. 267) may also arouse some sympathy in the reader.

GLOSSARY   **cobweb** fragile thing
                    beaten out defeated

CHAPTER 30

Why might Heathcliff ask Cathy about her feelings on seeing Linton's dead face?

Nelly has not seen Cathy since she left, although she has heard from Zillah, who dislikes what she sees as Cathy's proud behaviour. Zillah describes how Cathy tried to care for Linton but Heathcliff refused her any help and Linton died. In his will, everything, including what was previously Cathy's, was left to Heathcliff.

What signs do you notice of Hareton's feelings for Cathy?

Cathy was ill for two weeks, but eventually came downstairs. Hareton tried to befriend her, but she rejected him.

Nelly ends her story. Lockwood plans to tell Heathcliff he intends to spend the next six months in London and end his tenancy of the Grange after October.

COMMENT

Notice images of cold and death in the chapter.

Nelly warns that Zillah, who becomes the **narrator** (see Literary Terms), is 'a narrow-minded, selfish woman' (p. 268). Zillah portrays Cathy as haughty and disdainful, but the evidence suggests that Cathy is isolated and unhappy. Cathy says to Heathcliff: 'you have left me so long to struggle against death, alone, that I feel and see only death! I feel like death!' (p. 270).

GLOSSARY   **thrang** busy
                         fain glad
                         happen perhaps
                         starved frozen
                         stalled tired

CHAPTER 31

At the Heights, Lockwood delivers a letter from Nelly to Cathy. When Cathy complains her books have been destroyed by Heathcliff or stolen by Hareton, Lockwood suggests Hareton merely wanted to learn to read. Hareton then returns her books, but she refuses them. In frustration, he throws them on the fire.

Consider how the author makes us sympathise with Hareton in this scene.

Heathcliff seems changed and mutters about Hareton's increasing resemblance to Catherine. Lockwood announces he will be leaving the Grange, and departs.

COMMENT   Hareton pities Cathy and returns the letter she threw on the floor; he also returns her books. At the same time, he hates the way she mocks his attempts to read.

Heathcliff is haunted by Catherine. He sees her likeness in Hareton, and Lockwood notices his 'restless, anxious expression' (p. 279).

This change in Heathcliff foreshadows what is to follow.

Lockwood's reflection on how 'romantic' a relationship between Cathy and himself might have been seems out of touch with the reality of her feelings (p. 280).

GLOSSARY   **stalled** weary
                         Chevy Chase ballad of revenge and bloodshed between two
                         families

CHAPTER 32

Later that year (September 1802), Lockwood revisits the Grange to find Nelly has moved to the Heights. Arriving there, he notices a change in the atmosphere:

AN END AND A BEGINNING

Contrast this with Lockwood's description of the Heights in Chapter 1. there are flowers and fruit trees, and the gates and doors open to him. He sees a transformed Cathy and Hareton sitting together. Cathy is teaching Hareton to read, and Lockwood feels envious of their mutual affection.

He finds Nelly, who is singing, and Joseph, who is disgusted that Hareton has been bewitched by Cathy. In bringing Lockwood up to date with 'Heathcliff's history' (p. 285), Nelly explains how Heathcliff died the previous May after becoming more and more isolated, and how Hareton and Cathy became lovers.

COMMENT

The harmony between them is suggested by the description of 'her light shining ringlets blending, at intervals, with his brown locks' (p. 283).

This chapter shows the growing love of Hareton and Cathy which helps Hareton escape from the 'coarseness and ignorance' from which Heathcliff earlier predicted he would 'never be able to emerge' (p. 202).

The story of Hareton and Cathy is not unlike the fairy tale of *Beauty and the Beast*. When Beauty declares she will marry the Beast, he is transformed into a handsome prince, emerging from the spell cast on him by a wicked fairy. *Beauty and the Beast* first appeared in English in 1757, and appeared in a cheap popular book in the nineteenth century.

Books have previously caused conflict between Cathy and Hareton, but now they are a means of reconciliation through which Hareton becomes 'civilized' (p. 291).

GLOSSARY

bide live

They's nowt norther dry nor mensful there's nothing either dry or decent

Eea, f'r owt Ee knaw Yes, for all I know

Aw'd rayther, by th'haulf I'd much prefer

fellies men friends

jocks jugs (of beer)

Side out of t' gait get out of the way

bide it bear it

This hoile's norther mensful, nor seemly this place is neither
  decent or proper

we mun side aht we must get out

CHAPTER 33

Cathy and Hareton grow closer, planting flowers to replace Joseph's blackcurrant bushes. When Joseph complains, Cathy answers that Heathcliff shouldn't grudge her a garden when he has stolen all her and Hareton's property. Infuriated, Heathcliff attacks her, but then suddenly releases her, staring at her face.

Do you find this confession of Heathcliff's moving? Where else in the novel does he tell Nelly what he is feeling? (See Chapters 6 and 29).

One day, when they look up from their reading, Heathcliff finds their eyes resemble Catherine's. He says that although he has the power to destroy the houses of the Lintons and Earnshaws, the desire for revenge has gone. He senses a 'strange change approaching' (p. 297). He confesses extreme loneliness, and how in Hareton he sees not only a 'startling likeness' (p. 298) to Catherine, but also himself when young. Reunion with Catherine preoccupies him so much that he scarcely remembers to breathe.

COMMENT

His words recall Catherine's: 'He's always, always in my mind' (Chapter 9, p. 75).

Heathcliff reveals his inner feelings in poetic language that make it hard not to pity him: 'In every cloud, in every tree – filling the air at night, and caught by glimpses in every object, by day I am surrounded with her image!' (p. 298).

Nelly points out that nobody could tell Heathcliff's torment from his outward behaviour: 'You did not when you saw him, Mr Lockwood' (p. 299). She implies Lockwood might now see Heathcliff's behaviour in Chapters 1–3 differently.

GLOSSARY

Yah muh bend tuh th' yoak, an ye will you put up with this yoke,
  if you want

AN END AND A BEGINNING

> Aw'd rayther arn my bite ... wi' a hammer in th' road I'd rather
> earn my food as a labourer
> Aw sudn't shift fur Nelly – Nasty, ill nowt as shoo is I shouldn't
> move for Nelly – nasty good-for-nothing that she is
> quean girl
> een eyes
> E I
> riven pulled
> thick close together

CHAPTER 34

Different characters have different ideas of heaven. Does Heathcliff seem to have suffered in a kind of purgatory to achieve his?

In the April weather, Hareton and Cathy's gardening progresses. Heathcliff isolates himself, his behaviour strangely excited. He fasts for four days, telling Nelly: 'I am within sight of my heaven' (p. 302). On the third and fourth days, Nelly urges him to see a minister and the doctor. On the fourth evening, noticing Heathcliff's window is open, Nelly enters his room to find him dead. He is buried next to Catherine, with Hareton his only mourner. Since his death, local people claim to have seen him and Catherine together.

Nelly reveals Cathy and Hareton will be married on New Year's day 1803 and live at Thrushcross Grange.

Lockwood leaves, stopping at the church to see the graves of Heathcliff, Catherine and Edgar. The scene seems so peaceful, he wonders how anyone could imagine they should not be at rest.

COMMENT

We see the end of Heathcliff and his revenge against the Lintons and Earnshaws, and look forward to a new life for Hareton and Cathy. The flowers they grow and their marriage date (New Year's Day) emphasise their breaking away from the barren hatreds of the past, to make a fresh start.

Compare the deaths of Heathcliff and Catherine. Notice they both refuse food.

Heathcliff dies in the room he and Catherine shared as children, and in which Lockwood encountered Catherine's ghost. Heathcliff's hand is grazed by the window, recalling the ghost's hand in Chapter 3.

A detail linking Catherine and Heathcliff's deaths is Nelly's hearing of 'the murmur of the beck down Gimmerton' (p. 303). Just before Catherine's death, the same 'mellow flow of the beck' (p. 145) is heard from Thrushcross Grange. This suggests a link with Catherine's spirit and with the natural world they shared as children.

Lockwood says Catherine and Heathcliff must be finally at rest in their graves. Bearing in mind that local people say they have seen them on the moors, and remembering what they were like when alive, we may question this conclusion.

GLOSSARY

knock up make ill
Titan giant
hasped closed
harried carried
cut a caper dance
remembrance memento (here, money)

A   *Identify the speaker.*

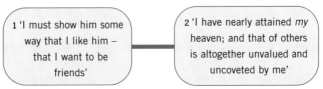

1 'I must show him some way that I like him – that I want to be friends'

2 'I have nearly attained *my* heaven; and that of others is altogether unvalued and uncoveted by me'

Identify the person 'to whom' this comment refers.

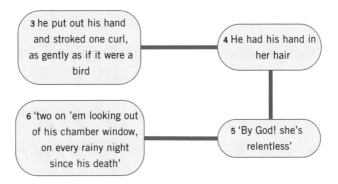

3 he put out his hand and stroked one curl, as gently as if it were a bird

4 He had his hand in her hair

6 'two on 'em looking out of his chamber window, on every rainy night since his death'

5 'By God! she's relentless'

Check your answers on page 92.

B   *Consider these issues.*

a How the developing love between Cathy and Hareton is portrayed.

b How the impression is conveyed of the change in Heathcliff, over his last four days, including the waning of his desire for revenge. Note any similarities between his and Catherine's deaths.

c Despite the brutality he has displayed earlier, and still displays towards Cathy (e.g. in Chapter 33), consider whether Heathcliff's revelations of his suffering (particularly to Nelly in Chapters 29 and 33) make you feel sympathy for him.

d At the end of the novel, whether you receive the impression that Heathcliff's death-defying wish to be reunited with Catherine is fulfilled. Note clues in the text that suggest this is the case.

PART THREE

COMMENTARY

THEMES

Wuthering Heights is rich in overlapping themes. Three major themes are:

- Love
- Revenge
- Death and the supernatural

LOVE

The main focus in the novel is the passionate, self-destructive love of Catherine and Heathcliff. Cathy describes her love, which is rooted in childhood, in Chapter 9: 'My love for Heathcliff resembles the eternal rocks beneath: a source of little visible delight, but necessary. Nelly, I *am* Heathcliff!' (p. 75). After Cathy dies, Heathcliff makes a similar declaration: 'I cannot live without my life! I cannot live without my soul!' (p. 155). Love is linked with dreams, through which Catherine finds the truth about her deepest feelings (Chapters 9 and 12). Also linked with love is the theme of separation and reunion. Heathcliff and Catherine experience this when Catherine stays at the Grange, then when Heathcliff leaves, and again at Catherine's death. Heathcliff dies convinced they will be reunited.

There are other kinds of love in the novel, including the love of parents and children in both Catherines' love for their fathers, and the mother-child relationship of Cathy and Linton. There is also the love of Frances and Hindley, without which he sinks into dissipation, and the love between Catherine and Edgar, which Nelly sees as 'deep and growing happiness' (p. 84) but which Catherine foresees changing 'as winter changes the trees' (p. 75). Finally there is the love between Hareton and Cathy, which frees Hareton from the prison of his ignorance and degradation and overcomes the destructive legacy of the past.

REVENGE

Heathcliff is not the only character who is vengeful. Early in the novel, Hindley wants revenge because he sees Heathcliff usurping his position. His persecution of Heathcliff sparks an answering, if hidden, desire for revenge which grows as Hindley's victimisation of Heathcliff increases. As Nelly says, it was 'enough to make a fiend of a saint' (p. 59).

Forced to work as a labourer by Hindley, Heathcliff deteriorates mentally and in appearance, whilst Catherine becomes 'the queen of the countryside' (p. 59). When Heathcliff overhears her say marrying him would 'degrade' her, he also hears her say she wouldn't have thought of marrying Edgar if Hindley 'had not brought Heathcliff so low' (p. 73). So it is Hindley along with Edgar, whose wealth and property Catherine finds so attractive, who separate Heathcliff from his love and inspire his pitiless revenge.

The themes of revenge and love are linked.

Heathcliff's revenge is to gain control of the property of the Earnshaws and Lintons with a view to destroying it. At the same time, he punishes the descendants of his enemies, subjecting Hareton to the same degradation that he himself suffered at Hindley's hands.

There is a sense in which Heathcliff becomes imprisoned in the isolation created by his obsession with revenge. Isabella and Cathy also both suffer imprisonment at his hands, and Isabella learns to want revenge, wishing she could 'take and eye for an eye, a tooth for a tooth' (p. 166). Cathy is more forgiving, though she still says she will have the 'revenge' of knowing that Heathcliff's cruelty arises from his loneliness and misery (p. 264).

DEATH AND THE SUPERNATURAL

How many of the characters are orphans?

Death is a common occurrence in *Wuthering Heights*, as it was in Emily Brontë's own experience, and the issue of what happens after death is one that runs through the novel. Nelly asks Lockwood, in connection with Catherine's death: 'Do you believe such people are happy in the other world, sir? I'd give a great deal to know' (p. 153). Different characters in the book have different ideas of heaven or hell, but it is the story of Heathcliff and Catherine that is most centrally concerned with this theme.

The novel contains different ideas about what happens after death.

The first two chapters of the novel contain references to the supernatural to prepare us for what comes later. We hear of fiends, fairies, the Black Art, a witch and a ghost. In Chapter 3, we encounter the supernatural in the form of Catherine's ghost which is given a powerful sense of reality. As we read on, the visit of the ghost is put in context.

Catherine talks about escaping from the 'shattered prison' of her body.

Even in her youth, Catherine says to Nelly, 'surely you and everybody have a notion that there is or should be an existence of yours beyond you.' (p. 75). And before Catherine's death, Nelly notices that her eyes seemed to gaze beyond the objects round her, 'you would have said out of this world' (p. 144). She anticipates a world where she will be 'incomparably beyond and above you all' (p. 148). After her death, Heathcliff asks her to haunt him: 'I know that ghosts *have* wandered on earth. Be with me always' (p. 155). In Chapter 29, he describes how he sensed her presence after her death, and how he has been haunted by her ever since: 'the moment I closed my eyes, she was either outside the window, or sliding back the panels, or entering the room' (p. 267). It is into this situation that Lockwood strays.

In the final chapter, Heathcliff experiences a change and is convinced that he has nearly attained his 'heaven' (pp. 302, 307) of being reunited with Catherine. The sightings of the couple by the locals after his death make us feel that he has achieved this heaven, and his end may be a beginning.

Note references in Chapter 34 which show Heathcliff's sense of being close to reunion with Catherine.

Death also involves a beginning in the case of Hareton and Cathy, whose births are both linked with the deaths of their mothers. Also, after Catherine struggles with death when Linton dies, she is brought to life again by her relationship with Hareton. Their love is linked with natural images (see Literary Terms) of growth (the garden they plant), and they are married at the birth of a new year.

STRUCTURE

HANDLING OF TIME

The novel reveals how the burden of events in the past has produced the 'present' situation.

Events in *Wuthering Heights* do not happen in chronological order. Lockwood describes the 'present' in his diary entry of November 1801, and finds it puzzling. To understand this 'present', we return to the past in a series of flashbacks (see Literary Terms) starting with Heathcliff's arrival in 1771, just over thirty years before. Then in the last few chapters, the story is carried forward to September 1802, and ends looking to the future.

Using the chart on p. 63 as a model, try to map the reader's journey through the rest of the novel.

One effect of this technique is to emphasise the influence of the past on the present, linking the fate of Heathcliff and Catherine with that of Cathy and Hareton. Also, by returning at key moments to Nelly and Lockwood in the 'present' (as after Chapter 9 when

FLASHBACK CHART

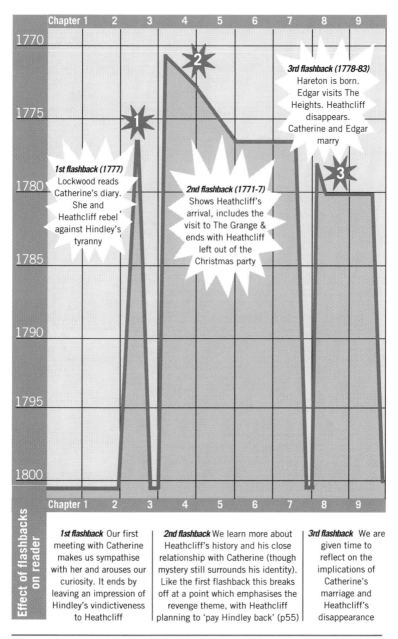

Chapter 1 2 3 4 5 6 7 8 9

1770
1775
1780
1785
1790
1795
1800

1st flashback (1777) Lockwood reads Catherine's diary. She and Heathcliff rebel against Hindley's tyranny

2nd flashback (1771-7) Shows Heathcliff's arrival, includes the visit to The Grange & ends with Heathcliff left out of the Christmas party

3rd flashback (1778-83) Hareton is born. Edgar visits The Heights. Heathcliff disappears. Catherine and Edgar marry

Chapter 1 2 3 4 5 6 7 8 9

Effect of flashbacks on reader

1st flashback Our first meeting with Catherine makes us sympathise with her and arouses our curiosity. It ends by leaving an impression of Hindley's vindictiveness to Heathcliff

2nd flashback We learn more about Heathcliff's history and his close relationship with Catherine (though mystery still surrounds his identity). Like the first flashback this breaks off at a point which emphasises the revenge theme, with Heathcliff planning to 'pay Hindley back' (p55)

3rd flashback We are given time to reflect on the implications of Catherine's marriage and Heathcliff's disappearance

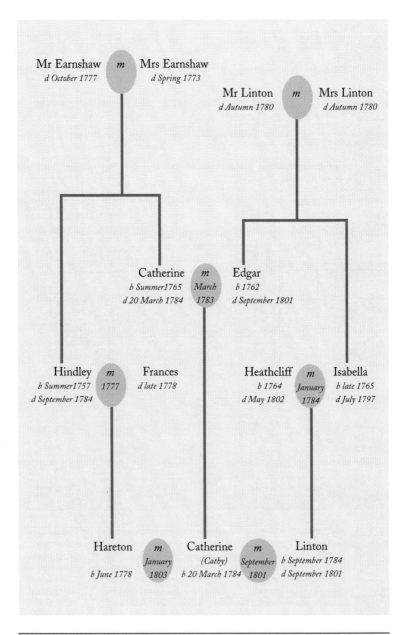

Mr Earnshaw **m** Mrs Earnshaw
d October 1777 *d Spring 1773*

Mr Linton **m** Mrs Linton
d Autumn 1780 *d Autumn 1780*

Catherine **m** Edgar
b Summer1765 *March* *b 1762*
d 20 March 1784 *1783* *d September 1801*

Hindley **m** Frances
b Summer1757 *1777* *d late 1778*
d September 1784

Heathcliff **m** Isabella
b 1764 *January* *b late 1765*
d May 1802 *1784* *d July 1797*

Hareton **m** Catherine **m** Linton
January *(Cathy)* *September* *b September 1784*
b June 1778 *1803* *b 20 March 1784* *1801* *d September 1801*

Heathcliff disappears), it breaks up the narrative and
allows us to think about the significance of events.

NARRATORS

*Advantages of
Emily Brontë's
narrative
technique.*

Lockwood is the main **narrator** (see Literary Terms),
telling us what Nelly Dean told him. She in turn tells
Lockwood what she has been told by other characters
such as Catherine, Heathcliff, Isabella and Zillah. This
makes the extraordinary events more credible, because
Lockwood is a highly educated observer. At the same
time, we get an insider's view from Nelly, who knows
the characters well. We can also share directly in the
characters' experiences and feelings, as with Heathcliff's
accounts in Chapter 6 and 29, Catherine's in Chapter
9, or Isabella's in Chapters 13 and 17.

*Unlike other
nineteenth-century
writers (e.g.
Charles Dickens or
George Eliot),
Emily Brontë does
not intrude to judge
her characters.*

Emily Brontë does not comment directly on her
characters, she shows us events through different
narrators, all of whom are limited or biased, so that we
have to make up our own minds. Her narrative
technique makes us aware that it is always possible to
see things from a different viewpoint, and, as well as
making the story more credible, increases our sympathy
with the main characters.

TWO FAMILIES

One aspect of the novel's structure is the symmetrical
pattern of relationships between the Earnshaws and
Lintons. At the start, both sets of parents have a boy
and a girl. Into this situation, Heathcliff, the outsider,
is introduced. The families are then linked through the
marriage of Catherine and Edgar. Here, we see the
significance of the names that Lockwood finds in
Chapter 3. Catherine Earnshaw, although she *should*
have become Catherine Heathcliff, becomes Catherine

Linton. She moves to the Grange with Edgar, then
after her death her ghost finally succeeds in returning to
Cathy and Linton the Heights with Heathcliff. In the second generation,
have their parents' Catherine Linton has to become Catherine Heathcliff
names, before she can be Catherine Earnshaw. She has to
underlining the move with Linton to Wuthering Heights, before finally
effect of the older being able to return to the Grange with Hareton. It is
generation on the as if the second generation is having to pay for the
younger. mistakes of the first. Cathy lives in reverse through the
pattern created by her mother, before achieving
happiness.

TWO HOUSES

The two families live in contrasting houses. As its name
suggests, Wuthering Heights is exposed to the wildness
of the elements, and its first generation characters are
associated with the 'heights' of passion. Thrushcross
Grange has gentler, more cultivated, perhaps Christian
('cross') **connotations** (see Literary Terms), and its first
generation characters are more civilised. In the second
generation, the contrast becomes blurred, as Cathy and
Hareton plant flowers from the Grange in their garden
at the Heights, and finally move to the Grange.

CHARACTERS

HEATHCLIFF

Heathcliff's Mr Earnshaw doesn't know what to make of the urchin
portrayal raises from the Liverpool slums: 'take it as a gift of God;
questions about though it's as dark almost as if it came from the devil'
him. What are his (p. 32). Later, Nelly asks Heathcliff: 'Who knows but
origins? Is he a your father was Emperor of China, and your mother an
man? a monster? Indian Queen ...?' (p. 51). Isabella asks whether he is a
a devil? 'devil', calls him 'a venomous serpent' (Chapter 13), and
describes him as a 'goblin' with 'cannibal teeth'

Shows endurance

Nelly describes

him as 'hard as

whinstone'(p. 30)

Passionately

devoted to

Catherine

Animal or

inhuman terms

often used by other

characters to

describe him.

His relentless

revenge bears out

Catherine's

description of him

as 'a fierce, pitiless,

wolfish man'

(p. 94).

(Chapter 17). Nelly reproves her by saying 'Hush, hush! he's a human being (p. 159), but even she describes him as behaving like a 'mad dog' (p. 149), then 'a savage beast' in his grief at Catherine's death (p. 155). In the final chapter, she muses: 'Is he a ghoul, or a vampire?' but although she admits this idea is absurd and influenced by horror stories, she is still left asking: 'where did he come from, the little dark thing, harboured by a good man to his bane?' (p. 303).

As a child, Heathcliff is called an 'imp of Satan' by Hindley (p. 35) but this is out of jealousy. One of Heathcliff's chief qualities under Hindley's brutal persecution is endurance, showing the hardness his name implies. Treated as a servant by Hindley, Heathcliff hears Catherine choose to marry Edgar with his wealth and social position, because marrying Heathcliff would 'degrade' her (p. 73). He leaves.

When he returns, he is transformed into a rich gentleman, as if to make himself worthy of Catherine. However, he sees both Hindley and Edgar as the cause of his separation from her and plans revenge. From then on, he becomes increasingly an oppressor. His revenge entails getting control of both the Earnshaws' and Lintons' property. As well as this, he mistreats Isabella and hangs her dog; he imprisons Cathy, is violent towards her and stops her visiting her dying father; he also callously punishes Hareton for Hindley's misdeeds.

Towards the end, Heathcliff's desire for revenge fades as he anticipates reunion with Catherine and sees her likeness in Hareton and Cathy. He dies in the room he shared with her, the window open, as though his spirit has joined her.

Emily Brontë invites us to see Heathcliff with compassion despite his brutality. This is done partly through portraying his early ill treatment, and giving Heathcliff's point of view, for example in Chapters 7 and 29. We are also influenced by Nelly's **ambivalent** (see Literary Terms), sometimes sympathetic comments. Finally, the idea that the devil has carried off Heathcliff is undermined as it is expressed by the hypocritical Joseph, who predicted the same fate for Cathy in Chapter 2. Joseph's final condemnation of Heathcliff has an alternative in the form of Hareton's grief.

CATHERINE EARNSHAW

As a child, Nelly says Catherine was always 'singing, laughing and plaguing everybody' but 'once she made you cry in good earnest, it seldom happened that she would not keep you company' (p. 37). She was a headstrong, mischievous but endearing child. Although she spits at Heathcliff at first, she becomes his ally, sharing the freedom of the moors with him and teaching him when Hindley stops his education. She says: 'My great miseries in this world have been Heathcliff's miseries, and I watched and felt each from the beginning' (p. 75).

Wilful and violent when thwarted Loyal to Heathcliff, but 'full of ambition' (p. 69) Wants to be 'the greatest woman of the neighbourhood' (p. 71)

After staying at the Grange, Catherine becomes more ladylike but still has a temper: she pinches Nelly and slaps Edgar in Chapter 8. Her attachment to Heathcliff remains, but the wealth and social position associated with marrying Edgar also attracts her. Catherine is honest and self-aware enough to admit her intuition that marrying Edgar is wrong, but convinces herself that it won't hinder her friendship with Heathcliff.

On Heathcliff's return, forced to choose between him and Edgar, she becomes ill with brain-fever. In her delirious state, she starts to understand her true situation, feeling a deep grief linked with separation from Heathcliff and being 'wrenched' from the Heights to be 'the lady of Thrushcross Grange, and the wife of a stranger' (p. 116). This supports Heathcliff's charge that she betrayed her deepest feelings when she chose social advancement by marrying Edgar. Catherine finally chooses to die, opening the window to expose her fever to the frosty air.

Capable of honesty and self-awareness. Her final death-wish is like Heathcliff's.

We see Catherine sometimes in a sympathetic, sometimes in an unsympathetic light. We witness her cruelty to Isabella in Chapter 10; we see her selfishness and wilfulness when she assumes Edgar must tolerate Heathcliff because she wishes it, and when she determines to break both men's hearts by breaking her own (Chapter 11); we are shown her undignified tearing of the pillow with her teeth (Chapter 12). At the same time, our sympathy is aroused by first meeting her through her childhood diary; by her loyalty to Heathcliff and moving expression of love for him (p. 75); and by her honest attempts at self-analysis in Chapters 9 and 12. Finally, the fact that Nelly misunderstands Catherine and underestimates her illness, dismissing her description of her love for Heathcliff in Chapter 9 and her painfully won insights in Chapter 12 as 'nonsense', increases our readiness to sympathise with her and see her as a **tragic** (see Literary Terms) figure.

HINDLEY EARNSHAW

Vengeful and violent towards Heathcliff
Affectionate to his wife, but leads a dissipated life after her death
Irresponsible father

Hindley's resentment of Heathcliff as an 'interloper' (p. 35), threatening his position as heir to the Earnshaw property, leads to violence as when he throws an iron weight at him. After Earnshaw's death, Hindley's treatment of Catherine and Heathcliff makes them rebel. He makes Heathcliff a servant, depriving him of education, branding him as a likely thief (Chapter 7) and undermining his relationship with Catherine.

After his wife's death, Hindley degenerates into
drinking and gambling. He drops Hareton over the
bannisters in Chapter 9 and, after Heathcliff's return,
deteriorates further. His gambling results in the
Heights being mortgaged to Heathcliff. Eventually, he
dies in suspicious circumstances, leaving his son and the
Heights under Heathcliff's control.

*Isabella describes
him as 'a tall
gaunt man ...
with masses of
shaggy hair' and
eyes which glare
'like a hungry
wolf' (p. 128).*

His importance lies in the fact that it is his degradation
of Heathcliff which makes Catherine choose to marry
Edgar and breeds Heathcliff's desire for revenge. He
also shows that Heathcliff is not the only vengeful
character in the novel.

Edgar Linton

*Contrast with
Heathcliff
Wealthy
Catherine finds
him handsome,
cheerful and rich
Caring husband
and father
Gentle
Civilised
Lacks spirit*

We first see Edgar, through Heathcliff's eyes, the
spoiled child of wealthy parents, squabbling with
Isabella. Later, Lockwood sees a portrait showing his
light hair, large eyes and 'almost too graceful' figure.
Nelly says 'he wanted spirit' (p. 60), and this shows in
his inability to leave after Catherine slaps him in
Chapter 8. Catherine marries him as he will own
Thrushcross Grange, socially the most important place
in the area. Whereas Heathcliff is an outcast from the
Liverpool slums, Edgar's family are landed gentry; his
background is cultivated.

*Compare Edgar's
reaction to
Catherine's
embraces (Chapter
10), with the
embrace of
Heathcliff and
Catherine
(Chapter 15).*

Edgar becomes a devoted husband, but where
Heathcliff is passionate, Edgar is restrained. Edgar has
conventional attitudes to social class, disapproving of
Catherine 'welcoming a runaway servant as a brother'
(p. 87). Whereas Heathcliff has no interest in
conventional religion, Edgar is a Christian (although
his disowning of Isabella is uncharitable), indeed he is
at Church during Heathcliff's final visit to Catherine
(Chapter 15).

As his health declines, Edgar tries to be protective towards Cathy but cannot resist Heathcliff's influence, even in the matter of his will. In contrast to the way Heathcliff uncovers Catherine's coffin, Edgar gently recalls his happiness in 'lying on the green mound' of her grave. He dies murmuring: 'I am going to her' (p. 261).

Edgar's marriage to Catherine is seen in different ways by different characters. On the one hand, Heathcliff claims Edgar 'is scarcely a degree dearer to her than her dog' (p. 138). Nelly, on the other hand, believes that, before Heathcliffis return, Edgar and Catherine 'were really in possession of deep and growing happiness' (p. 84). However, her view is biased in favour of her 'kind master' (p. 8). Catherine herself casts doubt on the happiness of the marriage by claiming that during Heathcliff's absence she endured 'very, very bitter misery' which 'that creature' (Edgar) knew nothing about (p. 91).

ISABELLA

At eighteen, she is 'a charming young lady ... infantile in manners, through possessed of keen wit, keen feelings, and a keen temper, too, if irritated' (p. 92).

Her childish infatuation with Heathcliff turns to hatred.

We first see her, aged eleven, squabbling with Edgar over a dog, crying because she cannot have what she wants. In the same way, in Chapter 10, she squabbles over Heathcliff with Catherine.

Having eloped with Heathcliff, she realises how wrong she was to idealise him as a 'hero of romance' (p. 139). Heathcliff's only interest in her is that she is Edgar's heir, so she is useful to his plan of revenge. After she is imprisoned at the Heights, other qualities in her character emerge. She, too, feels the desire for revenge and shows courage in opposing Heathcliff. Escaping from the Heights, she shows unlady-like energy, bounding over the moors, 'rolling over banks, and wading through marshes' (p. 168). After she flees

south, we hear of her giving birth to Linton, and finally
of her death.

CHATHERINE LINTON (CATHY)

High-spirited
Strong-willed
Loving
Forgiving
Shows courage in
standing up to
Heathcliff

She mischievously
puts primroses in
Hareton's porridge
(Chapter 33).

Cathy is like her mother with her 'capacity for
intense attachments'. In other ways, however, she
is unlike her. Nelly tells us 'her anger was never
furious; her love never fierce: it was deep and tender'
(p. 174).

Her independence makes her continue her relationship
with Linton against the wishes of Edgar and Nelly,
refusing to allow Nelly to be her 'jailer' (p. 224). Her
liveliness and energy show in her ideal way of spending
a summer's day, 'rocking in a rustling green tree, with a
west wind blowing … and the whole world awake and
wild with joy' (p. 229). Her affectionate and caring side
emerges when Edgar and Nelly are ill, and in her
compassion for Linton. Cathy feels a conflict between
her loyalty to her father and her pity for Linton, which
Heathcliff plays on. Despite her treatment by
Heathcliff, she is able to say: 'I know he has a bad
nature, he's your son, but I'm glad I've a better, to
forgive it' (p. 264).

She first misjudges Hareton, but after being reconciled,
their alliance under Heathcliff's oppressive regime
recalls her mother and young Heathcliff's alliance
against Hindley. After her mother's death, Nelly says
Cathy 'brought sunshine into a desolate house'
(p. 174), and the same is true of her influence at
the Heights. She creates a garden there, and through
her love, Hareton overcomes the malign effects of
Heathcliff's upbringing and his good qualities
blossom.

HARETON EARNSHAW

Sensitive
Generous
Forgiving
Loyal
Frustrated by
social degradation

We first see Hareton through Lockwood's eyes as a rustic clown: 'his thick, brown curls were rough and uncultivated, his whiskers encroached bearishly over his cheeks' (p. 9). However, even in Chapter 2 there are glimpses of his good nature as he offers to help Lockwood, and the more we understand him, the more our view of him changes. By the technique of using an inadequate **narrator** (see Literary Terms), Emily Brontë shows how easy it is to misjudge people.

Hareton is raised by Nelly until she goes to the Grange when he is five. Ten months later in Chapter 11. Nelly visits the Heights and meets Hareton, an elf-locked, 'brown-eyed boy' looking through the 'bars' of a gate (p. 100). She is shocked by the transformation in him as he throws a stone at her, stammers and curses. Heathcliff has prevented the curate from coming to teach him to read and write and boasts later of having 'tied his tongue' (p. 202). Hareton becomes the victim of Heathcliff's pitiless revenge on Hindley: to degrade Hareton as Hindley degraded him. Heathcliff boasts later that Hareton is 'gold put to the use of paving-stones' and that his good qualities are irretrievably 'lost' (p. 202). When he meets Cathy, Hareton tries to befriend her, but his uncouthness acts as a barrier and he is as frustrated when she prefers Linton, as young Heathcliff was when Catherine preferred Edgar.

An orphan, like
Cathy and
Heathcliff. Grows
up an illiterate
labourer, deprived
of his inheritance.

Despite Cathy's mockery and misjudgement of him (even to the extent of giving him a cut with her whip when he tries to make amends in Chapter 24), Hareton generously tries to befriend her and take her part. After he and Cathy are reconciled, he is transformed through their love in a way that recalls the fairy story of Beauty and the Beast. Hareton's good nature also shows in his grief for Heathcliff, whose loss of interest in revenge is associated with his seeing in Hareton 'a startling likeness to Catherine' (p. 298) and a similarity to himself.

LINTON HEATHCLIFF

Sickly
Spiteful
Selfish
Trapped by his
own bad nature

Selfishly gloats
that Cathy's
property will
become his
(Chapter 28).

Linton, 'A pale delicate, effeminate boy' (p. 185), has inherited the physical features of the Linton family without their redeeming qualities. When Cathy first meets him, she offers him tea in a saucer, 'like a baby' (p. 186) and indeed theirs is always a mother-child relationship. He lacks spirit though capable of futile rages as in Chapter 24 when, to Joseph's amusement, he threatens to kill Hareton for locking him in the kitchen, and ends by coughing blood. His idea of heaven, spending a summer day lying passively in the heather 'in an ecstacy of peace', contrasts sharply with Cathy's preference for a 'world awake and wild with joy' (p. 228).

Linton will 'undertake to torture any number of cats if their teeth be drawn' (p. 253). This pleasure in inflicting pain, reminding one of Heathcliff, also shows in his spiteful comments on Hareton's lack of education and his enjoyment of Cathy's distress in Chapter 23. He uses emotional blackmail to persuade Cathy to visit him, but repays her compassion by concealing Heathcliff's plan to trap her. He is unable to sympathise with Cathy when her father is dying.

Despite Cathy's pity for Linton it is hard to have much sympathy with him. Any that we do have might arise from his living in fear of Heathcliff, and his confession to Cathy: 'I am worthless, and bad in temper … I cannot help showing my nature to you, I regret it and repent it; and shall regret and repent it till I die!' (p. 234).

LOCKWOOD

Observant narrator but unreliable judge of character

Lockwood is perceptive, noticing details of setting and the characters' appearance and actions. However, as an outsider, he does not understand what he sees and is not a reliable interpreter or judge of character.

Outsider
Civilised
Educated
Can be pompous

Some readers may be put off by the style of the first three chapters, which may seem pompous and full of **Latinate** (see Literary Terms) vocabulary. But this is part of Emily Brontë's characterisation of Lockwood; there is something comic in his bewildered blunders in a world where people ignore the rules of polite society.

Emotional shallowness contrasts with capacity for deep attachments of lovers in the novel.

Why should Emily Brontë create a character like Lockwood to tell her story? One reason is that a story containing extraordinary events and extreme passions, is more credible if told by a civilised, educated outsider who is precise, even academic, in his observation of local **dialect** (see Literary Terms), meal times and architecture.

As well as being a civilised gentleman from the South, Lockwood is a man who avoids emotional commitment as we see in his response to the girl at the seaside. He vainly imagines Cathy might find him more attractive than Hareton, but his interest in 'the pretty girl-widow' (p. 29) is only a shallow romantic one, and he finally decides that a relationship with Cathy might disturb his 'tranquillity' (p. 236). Lockwood's name itself recalls his attempt to lock himself away behind the wooden bed panels from the turbulent, passionate world of the Heights. This avoidance of strong feelings, makes him a foil for those characters whose story he narrates.

A final **irony** (see Literary Terms) is that although we see how wrong Lockwood is in Chapter 1 to think he and Heathcliff are similar, there is a sense in which they are not unlike. The cruelty Lockwood shows in his dream suggests the underlying potential for violence in even the most civilised people, however much they may try to 'lock' away this side of their nature.

NELLY DEAN

Sees herself as 'a steady, reasonable kind of body' (p. 56)

Insider

Vivid reporter

Conventional

Limited understanding

First as nursemaid then as housekeeper, Nelly moves backwards and forwards between the Heights and the Grange. One of her advantages as a **narrator** (see Literary Terms) is that she is an insider who has known the characters since they were children. She also has an excellent memory for physical sensations, and for what characters said and did. This brings us close to the action and enables Emily Brontë to move us backwards and forwards in time.

Nelly is a graphic reporter of events; her language is full of homely phrases and vivid **images** (see Literary Terms and Language and Style). However, her unreliable judgement is shown on numerous occasions. For example, she mistreats young Heathcliff against Earnshaw's instructions; she delays telling Catherine that Heathcliff overheard her conversation; she keeps the seriousness of Catherine's illness from Edgar.

The name Dean suggests conformist moral and religious views.

Loyalty to Edgar makes Nelly's view of Catherine and Heathcliff biased. Her misunderstanding of Catherine's suffering and conflict in Chapters 11 and 12, and betrayal of her confidence make us feel sympathy for Catherine. She also increases sympathy for Heathcliff through her **ambivalent** (see Literary Terms) attitude. On the one hand, she condemns his brutality (for example to Cathy in Chapter 27) and criticises his 'selfish, unchristian life' (p. 307), on the other hand she sometimes invites compassion for him, recalling his childhood and asserting his humanity: "'Poor wretch!" I thought; "you have a heart and nerves the same as your brother men!"' (p. 154). The overall effect of her presence is that despite the unattractive sides to Heathcliff and Catherine, they retain our sympathy.

MINOR CHARACTERS

Joseph Hypocritical Calvinist who works for the Earnshaws. His use of Yorkshire **dialect** (see Literary Terms) helps establish a contrast between the Heights and the civilised world of Lockwood and the Grange. It also makes him an absurd figure, undermining the primitive religious judgement that Heathcliff is finally carried off by the Devil.

Zillah Housekeeper at Wuthering Heights. According to Nelly, 'a narrow-minded, selfish woman' (p. 268). A **narrator** (see Literary Terms) in Chapter 30, her judgement of Cathy is unreliable.

Mr Kenneth Local doctor. Hindley throws him in Blackhorse marsh.

Mr Green Lawyer bribed by Heathcliff to help him get control of the Lintons' property.

LANGUAGE & STYLE

The novel contains a variety of different styles, depending on which character is speaking. There are four main styles:
- The educated, literary style of Lockwood
- The vivid, often homely and colloquial style of Nelly
- The passionate language of Heathcliff and Catherine
- The local **dialect** (see Literary Terms) of Joseph

In addition to this, running through the whole book, is Emily Brontë's use of:
- The weather and seasons
- Key **images** (see Literary Terms)

Lockwood's style

Lockwood's is an educated, literary language, precise in its description of what he sees (e.g. his account of the Heights in Chapter 1). However, his style, with its large number of words of Latin origin, can also seem pompous and affected, as when he refers to Cathy as 'the beneficent fairy' (p. 11) or refers to Nelly and the servants as 'My human fixture and her satellites' (p. 28). He uses language to keep disturbing emotions at a distance, using Shakespeare's words rather than his own to describe how he 'never told' his love to the girl at the seaside (p. 4). His language emphasises that, both in social and emotional terms, he is an outsider.

Nelly's style

Nelly's style is homely, colloquial and vivid.

Nelly's language is colloquial as she talks to Lockwood: 'Hareton is the last of them, as our Miss Cathy is of us – I mean of the Lintons' (p. 30) and is full of idiomatic expressions and imagery (see Literary Terms). Heathcliff's history is 'a cuckoo's' (p. 30) and he is 'as uncomplaining as a lamb' (p. 34). Catherine is 'a little monkey' (p. 54) and the Lintons behave towards her like 'honeysuckles embracing the thorn' (p. 84). Nelly's language can be vividly descriptive, as when she describes Cathy on the moors musing over 'a bit of moss, or a tuft of blanched grass, or a fungus spreading its bright orange among the heaps of brown foliage' (p. 213).

At the same time, her language is sometimes not unlike the educated, genteel Lockwood's. For example, she says Heathcliff's 'naturally reserved disposition was exaggerated into an almost idiotic excess of unsociable moroseness' (p. 61). She puts this down to the influence of reading, but it also suggests her allegiance to the

world of the Lintons, and an adjustment of her
language for Lockwood's benefit.

THE STYLE OF HEATHCLIFF AND CATHERINE

*Recall his picture
of the bull-dog's
'huge, purple
tongue' and
readiness to smash
the windows 'to a
million of
fragments'
(p. 44–5).*

In describing their relationship or narrating past events,
the language of Heathcliff and Catherine is passionate
and vivid. This is seen in Heathcliff's description of
visiting the Grange in Chapter 5, his narrative in
Chapter 29 and his revelations to Nelly in the final
chapters. His account of how he sensed Catherine's
presence after her funeral is characteristic, with its
exclamations, short sentences, dashes and powerful
images: 'I looked round impatiently – I felt her by me –
I could *almost* see her, and yet I *could not* ! I ought to
have sweat blood then ...' (p. 266).

Their language is often poetic in its use of **imagery** and
rhythm (see Literary Terms) to convey feeling, as in
Catherine's description of her love for Heathcliff in
Chapter 9, with its natural images of winter, trees and
eternal rocks. Heathcliff speaks in a similar way, for
example in Chapter 33 when he describes seeing
Catherine 'In every cloud, in every tree – filling the air
at night, and caught by glimpses in every object'
(p. 298).

JOSEPH'S STYLE

By making Joseph speak Yorkshire **dialect** (see Literary
Terms), Emily Brontë suggests the remoteness of the
Heights from civilisation, and makes her story seem
more authentic, rooted in a traditional way of life. At
times, the broad dialect also makes Joseph seem rather
an absurd figure, as in his outrage at Catherine and
Heathcliff's treatment of his religious tracts: 'Miss
Cathy's riven th' back off 'The Helmet uh Salvation"
un' Heathcliff's pawsed his fit intuh t' first part uh

"'T' Brooad Way to Destruction!'" (p. 18). This
absurdity rubs off on to his rigid views on sin and
damnation, underlining the limitations of his
judgemental attitudes to other characters.

WEATHER AND SEASONS

Emily Brontë uses weather and the seasons to create
atmosphere (see Literary Terms), and reflect the
feelings of her characters. For example, after Heathcliff
runs away: 'There was a violent wind, as well as
thunder, and either one or the other split a tree off at
the corner of the building: a huge bough fell across the
roof' (p. 77). This emphasises the storm of feelings in
the characters concerned, and hints at the consequences
for the house of Earnshaw. Other examples of changes
in the weather are in Chapter 17 after Catherine's
death, and in Chapter 22 when Cathy's mood changes
after her meeting with Heathcliff: 'the rain began to
drive through the moaning branches of the trees, and
warned us to avoid delay … Catherine's heart was
clouded now in double darkness' (p. 216).

KEY IMAGES

Certain key images are repeated. See if you can find
other examples in these and other categories.

Windows

Windows suggest the existence of a barrier through
which a character can see something which they may
desire but from which they are separated. There are
many examples: the window in Chapter 3 through
which Catherine's ghost tries to enter; the window
through which Heathcliff and Catherine look at the
world of the Lintons in Chapter 6; the window through
which Heathcliff passes to visit Catherine's coffin in
Chapter 16; the open window through which it is

suggested Heathcliff has been reunited with Catherine in Chapter 34.

Gates, doors, locks and keys

These images emphasise the themes of separation and reunion, and imprisonment.

When Lockwood first visits the Heights, the gates and doors are shut, showing Heathcliff's imprisonment of Cathy and his self-imprisonment and isolation from the outside world. Both Catherine and Heathcliff lock themselves in their rooms before escaping from this world at their deaths. Cathy escapes from the protection of the park (Chapter 22), to find herself locked out, a prelude to her being locked in as a prisoner at the Heights (Chapter 27).

Animals

Note other examples of animal imagery used to describe characters.

Heathcliff is a 'pitiless, wolfish man' (p. 94). He is associated with the growling dogs in Chapter 1 and later gnashes 'like a mad dog' (p. 149). Here, and when Isabella is referred to as a 'tigress' in Chapter 10, the images suggest violence and aggressiveness. Other images suggest helplessness, as when Hindley is described as a 'stray sheep' (p. 99) and Edgar a 'sucking leveret' (p. 106).

Books

Books have different meanings for different characters.

They are frequently associated with education and culture. Edgar has a library, and Nelly has acquired her education through books. Cathy tells us Heathcliff 'never reads' (p. 276) and despite his burning of her books, it is through books that Hareton becomes cultivated and he and Cathy are brought together.

PART FOUR

STUDY SKILLS

HOW TO USE QUOTATIONS

One of the secrets of success in writing essays is the way you use quotations. There are five basic principles:

- Put inverted commas at the beginning and end of the quotation
- Write the quotation exactly as it appears in the original
- Do not use a quotation that repeats what you have just written
- Use the quotation so that it fits into your sentence
- Keep the quotation as short as possible

Quotations should be used to develop the line of thought in your essays.

Your comment should not duplicate what is in your quotation. For example:

> Nelly wonders if Heathcliff is a ghoul or a vampire and says she has read of such hideous incarnate demons: '"Is he a ghoul or a vampire?" I mused. I had read of such hideous, incarnate demons.' (p. 303)

Far more effective is to write:

> Nelly's view of Heathcliff is influenced by superstition and by books she has read: '"Is he a ghoul or a vampire?" I mused. I had read of such hideous, incarnate demons.'

However, the most sophisticated way of using the writer's words is to embed them into your sentence:

> Nelly wonders superstitiously if Heathcliff is 'a ghoul or a vampire', clearly influenced by the 'hideous, incarnate demons' she has come across in books.

When you use quotations in this way, you are demonstrating the ability to use text as evidence to support your ideas - not simply including words from the original to prove you have read it.

ESSAY WRITING

Coursework essay

Everyone writes differently. Work through the suggestions given here and adapt the advice to suit your own style and interests. This will improve your essay-writing skills and allow your personal voice to emerge.

The following points indicate in ascending order the skills of essay writing:
- Picking out one or two facts about the story and adding the odd detail
- Writing about the text by retelling the story
- Retelling the story and adding a quotation here and there
- Organising an answer which explains what is happening in the text and giving quotations to support what you write

....

- Writing in such a way as to show that you have thought about the intentions of the writer of the text and that you understand the techniques used
- Writing at some length, giving your viewpoint on the text and commenting by picking out details to support your views
- Looking at the text as a work of art, demonstrating clear critical judgement and explaining to the reader of your essay how the enjoyment of the text is assisted by literary devices, linguistic effects and psychological insights; showing how the text relates to the time when it was written

The dotted line above represents the division between lower and higher level grades. Higher-level performance begins when you start to consider your response as a reader of the text. The highest level is reached when you offer an enthusiastic personal response and show how this piece of literature is a product of its time.

Set aside an hour or so at the start of your work to plan what you have to do.

- List all the points you feel are needed to cover the task. Collect page references of information and quotations that will support what you have to say. A helpful tool is the highlighter pen: this saves painstaking copying and enables you to target precisely what you want to use.
- Focus on what you consider to be the main points of the essay. Try to sum up your argument in a single sentence, which could be the closing sentence of your essay. Depending on the essay title, it could be a statement about a character: Hareton's readiness to befriend Cathy despite her rejection of him, and his willingness to forgive Heathcliff and mourn his death despite the way Heathcliff treated him, show a good-natured generosity that Lockwood fails to appreciate at the start of the novel; an opinion about setting: The way the landscape surrounding Wuthering Heights is described in the first chapter reflects the stunted lives of its inhabitants; or a judgement on a theme: Love is the central theme of the novel, but the way the relationship of Heathcliff and Catherine is contrasted with that of Hareton and Cathy shows there is more than one kind of love.
- Make a short essay plan. Use the first paragraph to introduce the argument you wish to make. In the following paragraphs develop this argument with details, examples and other possible points of view. Sum up your argument in the last paragraph. Check you have answered the question.
- Write the essay, remembering all the time the central point you are making.
- On completion, go back over what you have written to eliminate careless errors and improve expression. Read it aloud to yourself, or, if you are feeling more confident, to a relative or friend.

If you can, try to type your essay, using a word processor. This will allow you to correct and improve your writing without spoiling its appearance.

Examination essay

The essay written in an examination often carries more marks than the coursework essay even though it is written under considerable time pressure.

In the revision period build up notes on various aspects of the text you are using. Fortunately, in acquiring this set of York Notes on *Wuthering Heights*, you have made a prudent beginning! York Notes are set out to give you vital information and help you to construct your personal overview of the text.

Make notes with appropriate quotations about the key issues of the set text. Go into the examination knowing your text and having a clear set of opinions about it.

In most English Literature examinations you can take in copies of your set books. This in an enormous advantage although it may lull you into a false sense of security. Beware! There is simply not enough time in an examination to read the book from scratch.

In the examination

- Read the question paper carefully and remind yourself what you have to do.
- Look at the questions on your set texts to select the one that most interests you and mentally work out the points you wish to stress.
- Remind yourself of the time available and how you are going to use it.
- Briefly map out a short plan in note form that will keep your writing on track and illustrate the key argument you want to make.
- Then set about writing it.
- When you have finished, check through to eliminate errors.

To summarise,
these are the
keys to success:

- **Know the text**
- **Have a clear understanding of and opinions on the storyline, characters, setting, themes and writer's concerns**
- **Select the right material**
- **Plan and write a clear response, continually bearing the question in mind**

SAMPLE ESSAY PLAN

A typical essay question on *Wuthering Heights* is followed by a sample essay plan in note form. This does not present the only answer to the question, merely one answer. Do not be afraid to include your own ideas and leave out some of those in the sample. Remember that quotations or close references to the text are essential to prove and illustrate the points you make.

In what ways does Emily Brontë make you sympathise with Heathcliff?

Introduction
The question involves recognising that Heathcliff is a problematic character who, because of his violence and brutality, might shock and repel readers, as indeed was the case for some contemporary reviewers. The 'ways' of the title involves looking at Emily Brontë's methods and techniques, and the effect of these in creating understanding and pity for Heathcliff.

Part 1
Heathcliff is portrayed in his childhood as having admirable qualities: courage, stoicism and loyalty. He is an orphan who mourns the death of his benefactor, and we are given examples of how he is victimised and degraded through the actions and language of Hindley.

Part 2
The author's use of Nelly as **narrator** (see Literary Terms) influences the reader's feelings about him. Despite her initial hostility and later disapproval of his actions, she recognises how badly he has been treated,

speaks up for his humanity to Isabella, and notices his suffering after Catherine's death and in the last chapters.

Part 3   Emily Brontë's narrative technique creates some chapters (6 and 29) where Heathcliff himself is the narrator. This lets us share his feelings and understand from Chapter 29 the unbearable anguish he was suffering which was not evident in Isabella's account of the events in Chapter 17.

Part 4   Emily Brontë gives Heathcliff a passionate language when he speaks of his relationship with Catherine. His appeal to her after her death in Chapter 16, his account of sensing her presence in Chapter 29, and his expression of his sense of loss in Chapter 33 make powerful use of poetic resources such as imagery and rhythm (see Literary Terms). This involves us in sharing his feelings.

Conclusion   Because we are shown Heathcliff's 'history' and childhood, because of the use Emily Brontë's narrative technique makes of Nelly and Heathcliff, and because of the language she gives to him, we do finally have some sympathy for Heathcliff rather than just condemning him from a position of critical detachment, as Joseph does after his death.

FURTHER QUESTIONS

Make a plan as shown above and attempt these questions.

> 1 "'Off, dog!' cried Hindley, threatening him with an iron weight used for weighing potatoes and hay. "Throw it," he replied, standing still, "and then I'll tell how you boasted that you would turn me out of doors as soon as he died, and see whether he will not turn you out directly."' (Chapter 4)
> How does the writer show the hatred between Heathcliff and Hindley here and later in the novel?

2 Wuthering Heights and Thrushcross Grange are very different houses. Compare them and the people who live in them. You may wish to consider the physical details and atmosphere of the houses the differences between people living there.

3 Give examples of different kinds of love relationships within the novel and comment on the characteristic qualities of each.

4 Show how important you feel the theme of *either* revenge *or* imprisonment is in the novel.

5 Examine the role played by dreams in the novel.

6 How much sympathy does the writer make you have for Catherine Earnshaw?

7 Compare the relationship of Heathcliff and Catherine with that of Hareton and Cathy.

8 Reread, in Chapter 24, the conversation between Cathy Linton and Linton Heathcliff on their different ideas of heaven. It begins: 'On my second visit, Linton seemed in lively spirits'. How does the writer create a contrast between Cathy and Linton here and in the rest of the novel?

9 Turn to Chapter 31 and read again the section beginning with Lockwood's '"No books!" I exclaimed' and ending with Hareton's exit. How does the writer portray the relationship between Hareton and Cathy in this section and later in the novel?

10 What do you find interesting about Emily Brontë's use of *either* locations *or* seasons and the weather in her novel?

11 How reliable, in your opinion, is Nelly Dean as a storyteller? You should consider at least two of the following, as well as any ideas of your own: her attitude and behaviour towards the first Catherine Earnshaw; her treatment of Heathcliff; her relationship with Edgar.

PART FIVE

CULTURAL CONNECTIONS

BROADER PERSPECTIVES

Film and
video

The 1939 film version of *Wuthering Heights*, starring Laurence Olivier and Merle Oberon (director: William Wyler), and the 1992 version (director: Peter Kosminsky) with Ralph Fiennes and Juliette Binoche both make changes to the plot, and play down the characters' unattractive sides. However, they do draw attention to certain features of the novel. The 1992 version, for example, emphasises the link between the generations and the similarity in situation between young Heathcliff and Hareton. There is a helpful critical guide on video by Literary Images Limited (Braceborough, Lincolnshire PE9 4NT).

Other works
by the Brontës

Emily Brontë's poems are widely available (e.g. *The Brontës: Selected Poems* ed. Juliet Barker, Everyman, 1993). As well as being worth reading for themselves, they contain the seeds of characters and themes in *Wuthering Heights* (e.g. those beginning: 'Cold in the earth'; 'Light up thy halls'; 'Well, some may hate, and some may scorn'). Charlotte Brontë's *Jane Eyre* (Penguin Classics, 1996 – first published 1847) portrays a school based on the notorious Cowan Bridge, and her *Shirley* (Penguin, 1974 – first published 1849) contains a character based on Emily.

Background
and biography

Phyllis Bentley: *The Brontës and their World* (Thames and Hudson, 1969), has illustrations of people and places; Winifred Gerin: *Emily Brontë* (Oxford University Press, 1971, paperback 1978) is interesting about influences on *Wuthering Heights*; both Edward Chitham's *A Life of Emily Brontë* (Basil Blackwell, 1987) and Juliet Barker's *The Brontës* (Weidenfeld and Nicolson, 1994) demolish Brontë myths, and are readable as well as impressively researched.

Criticism   The following contain a range of interpretations: *The Brontës: The Critical Heritage* ed. Miriam Allott (Routledge and Kegan Paul, 1984); *A Preface to the Brontës* by Felicia Gordon (Longman, 1989).

Novels based   Two absorbing novels about the Brontë family are:
on the Brontës *Dark Quartet* by Lynn Reid Banks (Penguin, 1976), and *Brontë* by Glyn Hughes (Black Swan, 1997).

ambivalence having two different views or feelings about the same thing

atmosphere mood

connotation implied meaning

dialect a variety of English with a distinctive vocabulary and grammar

flashback a sudden jump backwards in time to an earlier scene in the story

Gothic horror stories/novel kind of novel containing supernatural and macabre events, typically containing graveyards and ghosts. Popular in late eighteenth and early nineteenth centuries

image a word 'picture'

imagery language which creates a picture or image (e.g. through metaphor or simile)

irony saying one thing while meaning another. Where something has a meaning other than what is immediately apparent

Latinate of Latin origin

metaphor a comparison made by implication, without using 'like' or 'as'

multiple narration telling a story using more than one narrator

narrator the story teller

rhythm the movement or flow of the language

simile a comparison using 'like' or 'as'

symbol something simple which represent something else more complicated

tragedy story involving a character's suffering or downfall which moves us to pity the character despite their faults

TEST ANSWERS

TEST YOURSELF (Chapters 1–3)

A 1 Lockwood *(Chapter 1)*
2 Mrs Heathcliff (Cathy) *(Chapter 2)*
3 Catherine Linton (ghost) *(Chapter 3)*
4 Heathcliff *(Chapter 3)*
5 Heathcliff *(Chapter 2)*
6 Hareton Earnshaw *(Chapter 2)*

TEST YOURSELF (Chapters 4–9)

A 1 Hindley *(Chapter 4)*
2 Heathcliff *(Chapter 8)*
3 Catherine *(Chapter 9)*
4 Heathcliff *(Chapter 6)*
5 Catherine *(Chapter 6)*
6 Catherine *(Chapter 9)*
7 Heathcliff *(Chapter 9)*

TEST YOURSELF (Chapters 10–17)

A 1 Catherine *(Chapter 11)*
2 Catherine *(Chapter 15)*
3 Heathcliff *(Chapter 16)*

4 Heathcliff *(Chapter 10)*
5 Isabella *(Chapter 10)*
6 Edgar *(Chapter 11)*
7 Hareton *(Chapter 17)*

TEST YOURSELF (Chapters 18–28)

A 1 Hareton *(Chapter 21)*
2 Cathy *(Chapter 24)*
3 Linton *(Chapter 27)*
4 Heathcliff *(Chapter 27)*
5 Cathy *(Chapter 18)*
6 Linton *(Chapter 20)*
7 Hareton *(Chapter 24)*

TEST YOURSELF (Chapters 29–34)

A 1 Cathy *(Chapter 32)*
2 Heathcliff *(Chapter 34)*
3 Hareton *(Chapter 30)*
4 Heathcliff and Cathy *(Chapter 33)*
5 Catherine (Earnshaw) *(Chapter 34)*
6 Heathcliff and Catherine *(Chapter 34)*

GCSE and equivalent levels (£3.50 each)

Maya Angelou
I Know Why the Caged Bird Sings

Jane Austen
Pride and Prejudice

Harold Brighouse
Hobson's Choice

Charlotte Brontë
Jane Eyre

Emily Brontë
Wuthering Heights

Charles Dickens
David Copperfield

Charles Dickens
Great Expectations

Charles Dickens
Hard Times

George Eliot
Silas Marner

William Golding
Lord of the Flies

Willis Hall
The Long and the Short and the Tall

Thomas Hardy
Far from the Madding Crowd

Thomas Hardy
The Mayor of Casterbridge

Thomas Hardy
Tess of the d'Urbervilles

L.P. Hartley
The Go-Between

Seamus Heaney
Selected Poems

Susan Hill
I'm the King of the Castle

Barry Hines
A Kestrel for a Knave

Louise Lawrence
Children of the Dust

Harper Lee
To Kill a Mockingbird

Laurie Lee
Cider with Rosie

Arthur Miller
A View from the Bridge

Arthur Miller
The Crucible

Robert O'Brien
Z for Zachariah

George Orwell
Animal Farm

J.B. Priestley
An Inspector Calls

Willy Russell
Educating Rita

Willy Russell
Our Day Out

J.D. Salinger
The Catcher in the Rye

William Shakespeare
Henry V

William Shakespeare
Julius Caesar

William Shakespeare
Macbeth

William Shakespeare
A Midsummer Night's Dream

William Shakespeare
The Merchant of Venice

William Shakespeare
Romeo and Juliet

William Shakespeare
The Tempest

William Shakespeare
Twelfth Night

George Bernard Shaw
Pygmalion

R.C. Sherriff
Journey's End

Rukshana Smith
Salt on the snow

John Steinbeck
Of Mice and Men

R.L. Stevenson
Dr Jekyll and Mr Hyde

Robert Swindells
Daz 4 Zoe

Mildred D. Taylor
Roll of Thunder, Hear My Cry

Mark Twain
The Adventures of Huckleberry Finn

James Watson
Talking in Whispers

A Choice of Poets

Nineteenth Century Short Stories

Poetry of the First World War

Six Women Poets

Advanced level (£3.99 each)

Margaret Atwood
The Handmaid's Tale

William Blake
Songs of Innocence and of Experience

Emily Brontë
Wuthering Heights

Geoffrey Chaucer
The Wife of Bath's Prologue and Tale

Joseph Conrad
Heart of Darkness

Charles Dickens
Great Expectations

F. Scott Fitzgerald
The Great Gatsby

Thomas Hardy
Tess of the d'Urbervilles

James Joyce
Dubliners

Arthur Miller
Death of a Salesman

William Shakespeare
Antony and Cleopatra

William Shakespeare
Hamlet

William Shakespeare
King Lear

William Shakespeare
The Merchant of Venice

William Shakespeare
Romeo and Juliet

William Shakespeare
The Tempest

Mary Shelley
Frankenstein

Alice Walker
The Color Purple

Tennessee Williams
A Streetcar Named Desire

FORTHCOMING TITLES IN THE SERIES

Jane Austen
Emma

Jane Austen
Pride and Prejudice

Charlotte Brontë
Jane Eyre

Seamus Heaney
Selected Poems

William Shakespeare
Much Ado About Nothing

William Shakespeare
Othello

John Webster
The Duchess of Malfi

York Notes – the Ultimate Literature Guides

York Notes are recognised as the best literature study guides.
If you have enjoyed using this book and have found it useful, you
can now order others directly from us – simply follow the ordering
instructions below.

HOW TO ORDER

Decide which title(s) you require and then order in one of the following
ways:

Booksellers

All titles available from good bookstores.

By post

List the title(s) you require in the space provided overleaf,
select your method of payment, complete your name and
address details and return your completed order form and
payment to:

> *Addison Wesley Longman Ltd*
> *PO BOX 88*
> *Harlow*
> *Essex CM19 5SR*

By phone

Call our Customer Information Centre on 01279 623923 to
place your order, quoting mail number: HEYN1.

By fax

Complete the order form overleaf, ensuring you fill in your
name and address details and method of payment, and fax it
to us on 01279 414130.

By e-mail

E-mail your order to us on awlhe.orders@awl.co.uk listing
title(s) and quantity required and providing full name and
address details as requested overleaf. Please quote mail
number: HEYN1. Please do not send credit card details by
e-mail.

York Notes Order Form

Titles required:

Quantity	Title/ISBN	Price

Sub total _____
Please add £2.50 postage & packing _____
(*P & P is free for orders over £50*) _____
Total _____

Mail no: HEYN1

Your Name _____

Your Address _____

_____

Postcode _____   Telephone _____

Method of payment

☐ I enclose a cheque or a P/O for £_____ made payable to
Addison Wesley Longman Ltd

☐ Please charge my Visa/Access/AMEX/Diners Club card
Number _____   Expiry Date _____
Signature _____   Date _____

(please ensure that the address given above is the same as for your credit card)

Prices and other details are correct at time of going to press but may change without notice. All orders are subject to status.

☐ *Please tick this box if you would like a complete listing of Longman Study Guides (suitable for GCSE and A-level students)*

⬡ York Press

🅱 Longman

Addison
Wesley
Longman